EQUATOR

UGANDA   K E N Y A

EQUATOR

RWANDA

BURUNDI

ZAIRE

(CONGO)

TANZANIA
(TANGANYIKA)

ZANZIBAR

Z A M B I A

MALAWI

MOZAMBIQUE

call mama doctor

African notes of a young woman doctor

Louise
Jilek-Aall
M.D.

hancock

house

ISBN 0-88839-025-4
COPYRIGHT © 1979   Louise Jilek-Aall

Cataloging in Publication Data

Jilek-Aall, Louise, 1931-
Call mama doctor

ISBN 0-88839-025-4

1. Jilek-Aall, Louise, 1931-
2. Physicians - Africa, East - Biography.
3. Africa, East - Social life and customs.
I. Title.
R464.J54A3   610'.92'4   C79-091025-X

Design by Preston Denny

Photos and drawings by the author
unless stated otherwise.

Published simultaneously in Canada and the United States by:

 HANCOCK HOUSE PUBLISHERS LTD.
3215 Island View Road   SAANICHTON, B.C. V0S 1M0

HANCOCK HOUSE PUBLISHERS INC.
12008 1st Avenue South   SEATTLE, WA. 98168

Contents

To my mother Lily Weiser-Aall who
inspired my interest in anthropology
and folk medicine.

1
On the Way to Africa

The luxury liner *Kenya Castle* was plowing through Mediterranean waters on its way to adventure! A ship of the famous Cunard Line, she was sailing from England through the Suez Canal and the Red Sea down the African coast. Rounding the Cape she would return to Britain along the west coast of the African continent. I had boarded the ship in Genoa and would stay with her as far as Dar-es-Salaam, the capital of the then British Trust Territory of Tanganyika, East Africa.* It had been a great moment, standing on deck and seeing the hills of the old Italian city disappear at the horizon; my last glimpse of Europe perhaps for years to come. With the enthusiasm of an explorer I was looking forward to what lay ahead, the tasks awaiting me in the heart of Africa. At mid-twenty, already a medical doctor, I had recently obtained a diploma in tropical medicine. While I was completing this post-graduate training at the Swiss Tropical Institute of the University of Basel, I had been offered a research grant for the treatment of certain tropical diseases. Financed by the pharmaceutical companies which also employed me, the Swiss Tropical Institute maintained a small research center in the interior of Tanganyika

* Footnote: *Tanganyika and the island of Zanzibar were merged in 1964 to form the independent Republic of Tanzania.*

some 600 miles south of the equator. There the Roman Catholic mission had built a large hospital that worked in close cooperation with the research center. In order to survive on my small grant, I had contracted to render medical services to the many outposts of the Catholic missions in the diocese of Dar-es-Salaam where my work would be. The area extended from the coast of the Indian Ocean into the southeastern part of the country and included the Ulanga district with several mountain ranges as well as the districts of Kilwa and Nachingwea. Since I was neither Catholic nor missionary it was quite generous of the Archbishop of Dar-es-Salaam to accept my request. Without our mutual service it would not have been possible for me to live in the African bush.

Under deck, in the ship's storage room, was the huge wood trunk with the chemical ingredients and scientific instruments I needed for my research. It had been a struggle to get the mysterious trunk through the Italian Customs. To my great alarm the Customs officers were not inclined to believe that the upset young woman before them was a real *dottore* and that the trunk contained nothing but legitimate equipment. I fought desperately against their intention to break open the big case as it would have disturbed the well-balanced manner in which the numerous glass retorts, the microscope and the highly sensitive instruments had been packed. Not before I had stirred up enough fuss for a highly placed official to intervene did they give up and clear the huge trunk unopened. In a last minute scuffle the trunk and myself were hustled on board the ship which was about to put out to sea.

Still excited from nearly having missed the boat I inspected the tiny cabin which was to be my private room for weeks to come. To live up to my firm intention to study the Swahili language I would need in Tanganyika, I at once placed my books on the table beside the bed. With a feeling of joy I arranged the cabin. Having finished this, I went to the dinner table full of curiosity about my fellow passengers. I listened eagerly to their talk of Africa and asked all sorts of questions. Most of the people at the table turned out to be colonial

8

officials and government employees returning to their posts after a holiday in Britain. With my inflated ego and explorer's enthusiasm I became an annoyance to them, and they showed their feelings, looking down their noses and giving the cold shoulder to my naive questions. They seemed to belong to that unhappy category of civil servants who hate serving overseas and continuously dream about returning to Britain. But having become used to being treated as important persons, as *bwanas* with subordinates, servants and houseboys, they find it hard to fit into everyday life at home. They cannot find a place to function there and return disillusioned to their boring life in the colony. These people talked about Africans with contempt, reporting petty incidents and relating stereotyped stories which seemed only to reflect their own resentment. On board the English liner they were determined to get as much fun as possible out of the trip as long as they were still in a "civilized" environment. But their way of having fun was quite foreign to me. I realized that I had been too immersed in my medical training to know what life was like outside university circles.

A painful blunder in my attempts to make social contact came on the second day on board. We had all received an invitation from the ship's captain to attend a cocktail party the next afternoon at 2:00 p.m. I had never heard of such a party before. *Cock-tail* party? It sounded slightly indecent to me and I naively asked a group of young people who had begun to show some mild interest in me what such a party implied? My question gave rise to general hilarity. Now they had found something to tease me about and they used it mercilessly. They vowed to show this oddball of a girl how normal people have fun together. They dragged me into the bar and asked me for my favorite drink: Singapore Sling?—Pimm's No. 1?—Whiskey Mac? My ears buzzed with weird names. How could I tell the laughing people that I did not know any of these drinks? So far, I had not discovered that it was necessary to drink in order to be socially acceptable. I certainly did not dare to drink much now, as I would very quickly make an even greater fool of myself than I already had. In an unobserved moment I slipped outside and stood at the railing letting the fresh air cool my burning face. I actually felt like a coward for having fled the bar like this. As I stood there looking out into the dark, my self-pride came tumbling down. I felt uneasy and slightly ridiculous. Here I was, a "romantic," fresh-baked doctor and specialist in tropical medicine on the way to challenging adventures in the African bush, who did not even know how to handle a bunch of exuberant fellow passengers. My high-spirited mood left me and I felt lonely there in the dark.

A young sailor came up to me and greeted me shyly. Did I know that the ship was nearing the island of Sicily and that in passing it we would be able to see the glow of the volcano Etna, he asked in a friendly voice. Thankful for having been lifted out of my brooding, I asked him about the volcano. I looked out for it through the dark and after a while thought I could see a faint gleam far away. "Is that the volcano?" I turned around to the friendly sailor, but he was gone.

How dark it was! The shining crests of the waves reflected the lights of the ship and then disappeared again into obscurity making the night look even darker. Was this darkness not like the uncertain future awaiting me in Africa? I could not look through it; I did not know what was in store for me there. Now the faint light of the volcano was becoming clearly visible. It glowed like a red eye between heaven and earth out there. In ancient times volcanoes were sites of the Gods; Christianity made them into glowing messengers from Hell—sinister warnings of destructive powers in the depths of the earth. The glimmering light which seemed to pulsate through the dark night sent feelings of awe and fear into the human heart. If the immense powers should ever break loose all the waters of the oceans would not be enough to extinguish the infernal fire. I stood there in complete self-forgetfulness, engulfed in the mystery of the elements: earth, fire, water and air. A premonition of the drama of Life and Death which I was to experience in Africa filled me with a sense of purpose.

2
Road-Users in the Bush

Before the *Kenya Castle* arrived in Tanganyika I had reached a kind of truce with my teasers on board. They had given up trying to make me drink, and as I spent much of the time studying in my cabin, they soon forgot about me. When the ship moored in Dar-es-Salaam, I was met by a Capuchin priest in a white habit who came to the gangway to greet me and give me a hand with my bulky luggage. As we drove into town, I eagerly took in the exciting scenes of life in Africa. Dar-es-Salaam in the 1950's was still a typical colonial city. The main buildings were schools, churches, hotels and curio shops. Outside the "New African Hotel," built in the German colonial style of the Kaiser's period, sat the white *bwanas* in their khaki suits, sipping drinks and being served by fancy-dressed African "boys." There were only a few cars in the streets. Crowds of barefoot people in long robes walked along, carrying merchandise on their heads and small children on their backs.

We drove to the Archbishop's House where my big trunk would await transport into the interior and I was taken across the street to the Catholic school compound where the lay teachers occupied one wing of the convent with a few extra rooms for guests. They were friendly and during mealtime showered me with stories and well-meaning advice on how to survive in Africa. My excitement and expectation grew the more I listened and I found it hard to sleep at night. The heat was oppressive and a thousand unfamiliar noises from the street also kept me awake. This time of the year the atmosphere on the coast was saturated with humidity. At night water condensed on the roofs, dripping monotonously onto the pavement. My sheets and clothes were damp, and the sweat, which could not evaporate, simply ran off my skin. Being unaccustomed to the tropics, I found the heat nearly unbearable, especially during the noon hours. Unable to find a way to cool off, nauseated and with an aching head, I had to give up doing anything. I lay flat on my bed desperately longing for the sun to set and wondering whether I would ever be able to tolerate this climate. The teachers, noticing my suffering, consoled me as best they could. It would be less humid in the interior they assured me, and it would even cool off during the night. Needless to say I waited impatiently for my departure to Ifakara, the small town in the Ulanga district lying about two hundred miles inland from the coast where the research center at the Catholic mission hospital was situated.

Finally the day came; a message arrived that we were to start out at 2 o'clock the next morning. I felt like a real adventurer as I quietly locked the heavy iron gate of the convent behind me and threw the key back into the yard as instructed. The stars shone with startling brightness. I could hear the motor of the waiting truck as I crossed the empty streets. In the glare of the headlights I greeted the driver, a Capuchin friar from Switzerland. I could distinguish my wooden trunk amidst the load on the truck. Half a dozen boys were sitting on it; they were to come along with us. The truck would hardly ever make more than thirty miles per hour on the poor bushroads, and many times during the day I wished I could have joined the boys back there as I sat squeezed in between the driver and a mother with her baby riding with us inside.

The first hours of driving through the night were fine. The air was cool and pleasant and saturated with the aromatic scent of the shrubs and plants alongside the road. Gradually the stars faded away as dawn lit up the sky. The morning clouds glowed red and gold and I sat spellbound as the African landscape unfolded in the morning sun before my eyes. Never had I seen anything so beautiful: the rolling hills stretched for miles ahead; the distant Kilosa mountains showed dark blue against the purple sky; the bao-bab trees reached with their silvery branches like hands into the air. On the reddish-brown soil of the wide steppe I saw herds of zebras and antelopes grazing peacefully. The immensity of the land deeply impressed me and I felt in my heart that whatever lay ahead, I would always be happy for having lived in Africa.

As the day went on and the sun climbed higher, the heat in the truck intensified. It became more difficult to sustain a joyful mood. Drowsiness overwhelmed us. The mother and her baby slept soundly even though their heads were banging against the sides of the cabin as the truck bounced on the bumpy road. Alarmed, I noticed that the driver too was struggling to keep his eyes open as he steered the heavy truck along a winding road through the forest. I forced myself to stay awake, asking questions and cracking jokes just to keep him alert. We had just turned off the paved road at Morogoro and were driving on the dirt road towards Mikumi when suddenly the driver jammed on the brakes and switched off the motor. The truck stopped dead, clouds of dust rising up from the wheels. He put his arm across me and whispered, "Don't move!" Through the dust I perceived a huge grey mass in front of the truck. We had just rounded a bend on the road and it was a few seconds before I realized that we were facing an elephant. It slowly lifted its trunk and swung its head from one side to the other as it searched for the smell of the unexpected intruder. None of us in the truck dared to move or make a sound. The elephant seemed immense as it raised its ears ready to charge at the slightest further provocation. Then the elephant slowly turned away and walked off into the bush, crushing branches as it went. With a sigh of relief the friar started up the truck again.

We were now wide awake and could hear the excited voices of the boys in the back. The driver told me of cars coming too close or hitting an elephant. The infuriated beast is able to smash a car and will charge people who try to flee the scene. Newcomers to Africa who panic and run headlong into the bush have little chance to escape since the elephant is a much faster runner. Seizing its prey with its trunk the elephant will throw the victim up in the air and then crush him under its heavy feet. Those who know better will run a zig-zag course because the elephant in motion cannot stop to turn quickly. Once out of the view of the animal the trick is to lay motionless in a ditch or behind a bush. Fortunately elephants have poor eyesight. To them things which do not move or make a noise have no meaning, especially if there is no irritating smell. If the wind is favorable the elephant, guided mainly by smell and movement, will lose track and quickly give up the chase. "The best protection against such dangerous encounters is to drive slowly," concluded the friar.

In the early afternoon we stopped at a small village to let the woman with her baby get out. The cabin was more spacious now and more comfortable. But soon the sun burning through the window made us drowsy again. The driver stopped the truck at the roadside. This was his favorite picnic site, he said, as he helped me out, and here we were going to have lunch and take a rest. He brought along his safari-box with food and tea and went to a beautiful place under some old trees. We sat down on a stump. "What about the boys?" I asked, a bit concerned. "The people in the bush never eat meals during daytime," the friar explained. "They take a few sticks of sugar cane with them on trips and whenever they feel the need, they cut off a piece and chew it. The sweet juice quenches the thirst and is nourishing at the same time. In that way they keep alert without becoming heavy with food."

While we were resting in the cool shadow of the trees the friar told me about his work. He had been driving this same route for many years and knew the road like his own pocket. During long hours of driving he had come to know many different kinds of people. Within the confines of the truck he had met with persons who were quiet, thoughtful, preoccupied, or even depressed, while others were gay and talkative. Sometimes the passengers were nervous and would be impatient with his slow driving, at other times they were in harmony with themselves and therefore appreciative of his caution. He had made it a habit to size up his passenger at the beginning of the trip and to plan the day accordingly. Allowing his companion time for rest and sleep when that seemed necessary, he would at other times kindle a conversation, especially when he himself felt a tendency to doze off. To keep the passenger talking he had a repertoire of themes of which he would choose one, depending upon whether he had a priest, a nun, a physician, a nurse or a teacher in the truck, the friar revealed with a laugh. For a moment I felt uneasy, wondering in what category I had been placed, but our conversation was flowing with such ease and humor I could not possibly believe that it was calculated. As we drove on I listened to him in silence and together we enjoyed the splendor of a tropical sunset and watched darkness descend on the plains. When we finally reached Ifakara late at night I felt that this Capuchin friar had become my first true friend in Africa. Whenever I thought of him in the years to come the little figurine of St. Christophorus which dangled above the dashboard in his truck came to my mind. I always tried to arrange it so that I could travel with him when I had to go to the Coast. The journey was never the same if he was not the driver.

3

Becoming Mama Mganga

It was the first morning in my new room. I woke up from a restful sleep such as I had not enjoyed for a long time. It was indeed nice and cool here, compared with the sweltering climate of the coast. I had gone to sleep wondering about the swarm of hungry mosquitos hovering outside the net around my bed. There seemed to be thousands of them, and the buzz of their wings blended into a high-pitched monotonous song which helped me fall asleep. Now, looking through the window beside the bed, I could see where they had come from; there was neither glass nor protective screen and the fresh morning air gently stroked my cheeks. From the bed I could see the two towers of the church across the yard. "A—e—i—o—u, ma—me—mi—mo—mu"; it was a chorus of children's voices. I sat up in bed and looked outside. Beside the church was a small school house, or rather an open shed. I could see the curly-haired heads of the little children sitting in rows and facing the teacher, who was standing with his back to me, swinging his arms like a conductor. The sweet voices of the children taking their first English lessons were to wake me every weekday morning as long as I stayed in Ifakara.

My room was tiny; there was hardly any space between the bed, a table and chair and the old clothes cupboard. A small veranda gave me more freedom to move, but during the daytime it was too hot out there and at night the mosquitos made it impossible to sit anywhere but under the mosquito net. Downstairs was the dining room. Food was provided by the convent of which this old house was a part. The mission was in the process of building a new wing onto the convent, so the old house was allowed to dilapidate—and dilapidate it did! Every night bats and crows fought endless battles under the roof. With blood-curdling shrieks and loud scratching of claws and wings they rumbled above my head, sending down dung and dust from the ceiling. A layer of it covered everything in the room and had to be cleaned off every morning. I used to hold my breath when scooping up the mess; the awful stench of the bat manure made me retch. I do not think anybody knew the dreadful condition the room was in; it had been unoccupied for a long time, and nobody ever visited me there. Most of the day I spent in the hospital anyway, so I did not make a fuss about it.

On the first day, I began to unpack my equipment and to install myself in the research institute. But very soon my good intentions gave way to paralyzing frustration. I was simply unable to work. The unfamiliar environment, the many new faces, the language problem and the fact that the hospital staff was too busy to take time to explain things to me, made me feel like I was in a daze. How foolish one appears when unable to speak the language! I caught myself hiding in my lab, too embarrassed to venture through the hospital for fear of having to respond to questions. It was a shattering experience to find out that the Swahili I had taught myself on the ship was of so little value in real life.

The hospital complex, consisting of one-storey brick buildings, was spread out over a large area, each wing connected by a roofed walkway. The wards were always overcrowded and sometimes patients shared their beds with family members. Others slept on mats on the floor between the beds.

I could not make out who were the patients and who were the relatives or visitors. In the evenings people were sitting around small fires everywhere on the hospital grounds, cooking food for themselves and for their sick. The people would watch me with curiosity and laugh at my clumsy attempts to communicate with them. In my desperation I went to see the head nurse, an old nun who had worked at the hospital since it was founded some thirty years ago. Everybody in trouble turned to her, I was told. She listened patiently to my problems and at once had a plan ready. "Forget about your research for a while," she said. "First learn about the people and their illnesses and acquire enough knowledge of Swahili to handle the patients." She suggested that I start off by working in the hospital laboratory; the technicians spoke some English and could teach me Swahili whilst I worked with them. Moreover she invited me to spend the first morning hours with her as she conducted the out-patient clinic.

Sitting there beside her under the protection of the great prestige and respect she enjoyed, I finally felt at ease and began to grasp what was going on around me. Every patient coming to the hospital had to be screened at the out-patient clinic. Sitting at a long table with all kinds of medicines in front of her, the nurse examined each patient and decided what had to be done. With a score of helpers she was able to handle hundreds of patients everyday. Some received their routine medication, others were sent to the laboratory for tests, again others were referred to the dressers for injections or wound treatment or for fitting of casts. Those who appeared seriously ill might be sent for X-rays or other investigations and only a few had to be directed to the waiting room of the hospital's only physician. There they might wait for hours until the busy doctor could find time to examine them between operations and in-patient visits.

The technicians in the laboratory at first did not know how to deal with me and it took quite some time before they overcame their initial apprehension. I had to explain to them over and over again why I was there, how life had been in

18

Europe and why I had come to Africa. As they later admitted, it was only after I had passed their secret tests, such as sharing some food with them, helping them work overtime and laughing at their jokes, that they accepted me on an equal footing. Once that was achieved, they rivaled one another in teaching me Swahili and in telling me about their life in the bush. I could never thank the old nun enough for having guided me so well during this first month of my stay in Africa. Not only did I become versed in diagnosing the different kinds of bacteria, worm ova and parasites we daily discovered under the microscope, I also learned much about the people, their beliefs and customs from the three technicians. But that was not all; the head nurse took me along to assist her on the maternity ward where she attended to her favorite call—midwifery. With enormous experience, skill, and firm hands she delivered babies and trained young mothers to take care of their newborn.

I soon developed confidence in delivering babies and assisting her with complicated cases and she arranged for a small room at the entrance to the maternity ward where I began to see patients she sent me from the out-patient clinic with the non-infectious diseases I was to treat in my research project. At the same time I could keep a watchful eye on the expectant mothers. I liked it so well there that instead of returning to my bat-dung infested room in the convent I stayed on in the hospital until late at night. Since I was not part of the regular hospital staff and could set my own pace, I never discouraged visitors. People soon discovered this and liked to drop in, even if it was just to sit on the floor and watch me work. Sometimes one of the boys from the laboratory would join me there after work, helping me to translate what people said or telling me what was going on in the hospital. My room on the ward eventually became a meeting place in the evenings after the hospital staff had left. Only African personnel worked on the wards during the night. One European nurse was on duty and stayed in a house close enough to the hospital to be quickly at hand if called.

Amazing how the whole atmosphere in the hospital changed at nighttime! It was like two different worlds: the rational, highly organized world of the European physician and nurses dominating the scene and instilling confidence during the day, and the mystical, anxiety-charged world of the African bush taking hold of the people during the night. When the European staff left, dangerous spirits and the power of magic filled the darkness. People huddled together and discussed the events of the day. They thought of anesthesia as "making a person nearly dead" and the surgeon who could operate on the patient and make him come back to life again was a great magician charged with astounding powers. The people loved and feared him at the same time. If a patient did not recover as quickly as they expected, fear and suspicion would flare up. The relatives would anxiously go over what the doctor had said or done. Had the doctor smiled at the patient or frowned at him? Was he displeased in any way? Why did the patient not improve? Surely somebody must be responsible. Messengers were sent back to the village telling the medicine man about the patient's condition and asking for advice. Worried people taking refuge in my room whispered about poisoning and witchcraft. Maybe the neighbor who never came to visit was using black magic against the patient. Or perhaps the evil influence came from the patient in the next bed who was of a different tribe. Even though I did not understand everything too well, I felt the constant emotional stress the people lived under. It opened my eyes to a world of anxiety and I always remembered that part of the lives of the people whom I later was to treat in the bush.

Sometimes the medicine man would advise the family that the patient could only recover if taken home. Then the people would become extremely agitated and after debating for hours might pack up and sneak the patient out of the hospital in the dark. The same could happen if the patient felt he was going to die. People were afraid of dying in the hospital, I was told. They wanted to be at home where the proper death rituals could be performed. Much to the physician's dismay, it

20

happened that a seriously ill patient under intensive care had disappeared by the time of the morning rounds. Silence would meet the upset doctor; nobody dared to tell him that the family had taken the patient home to the village because they were convinced that he was going to die.

I had been completely absorbed in my work at the hospital for a few weeks when one day my friend the Capuchin truck driver asked to see me. He waited at the hospital entrance with a bicycle. "I think it is a pity that you bury yourself in the hospital," he said. "Why don't you look around a bit? Here, take my bike and go on trips sometimes," and with a broad smile he handed the bicycle to me. A warm feeling of gratitude filled me when I was riding along seeing people live and laugh in the villages. He was right; I had forgotten life was going on outside the hospital walls. With joy I saw that some people recognized me. They shouted, *"Jambo, Mama Mganga*—How are you, Mama Doctor?" By now I knew how to answer, *"Mzuri, asante sana*—Very well, many thanks," as I passed them on the bike. *Mama Mganga* was the name I became known by in Tanganyika. As a matter of fact I never heard my personal name for years.

One evening after work I again set out on the bike. I had been told of a bush fire burning somewhere in the vicinity and I wanted to have a look at it. I knew my way through Ifakara, but then the road turned off into the bush and became quite narrow. Without hesitation I kept up speed, enjoying the head-wind I created. Soon the sun was setting behind the trees, and the fire was still far away out on the plains. Should I dare go on? Perhaps a little further on I would have a good view of the fire. Suddenly I heard the rumble of many galloping animals; it seemed to come right in my direction. I jumped off the bike and looked around for somewhere to hide. But there was no time. A large gnu-antelope broke out of the bush right in front of me, followed by a horde of others. I stood frozen as the animals rushed towards me. There was a ditch at the roadside; the first animal cleared it with an elegant leap and all the others followed. One after the other they threw their heads

21

back and jumped, their horns nearly touching their backs. They flew through the air, landing with ease on the other side, and continued their fleeting gallop without the slightest change in speed. What a sight! The strong smell of warm animal bodies increased the impression of power and speed. As I stood there dumbfounded I heard the stampeding of more animals. They were fleeing from the approaching bushfire. What if there were elephants among them? It suddenly dawned upon me that I was in danger. I turned the bicycle and fled in the same direction as the animals, away from the fire.

There was a fork in the road which I had not seen on my way out. But there was no time to choose, I just hoped I took the right path. It was getting dark fast and I was alone in the bush with running animals all around me. I could see pairs of eyes flashing in the reflection of my dynamo light. It nearly scared me out of my mind, but I did not dare to stop because then the bicycle lamp would go off and I would be completely in the dark. I worked the pedals as fast as I could, holding on to the bike and desperately hoping I would soon reach a village. I must have taken the wrong way because the road seemed to lead nowhere. I began to feel exhausted; how long could I keep up the wild speed? But the sound of the fleeing animals drove me on and I pedaled with pounding heart and burning eyes. Just as I thought I could not make it any further I saw light through the trees. The road made a turn and ended in a court yard. A man was standing in front of a house looking out in the direction of the fire. He got a scare as I came racing into his yard and half fell off the bike, shaking and panting, unable to utter a word.

"Good gracious, young lady, what's the matter? What are you doing out here at night?" It was asked in English. "I...I wanted...to see...the fire," I stuttered, still out of breath. "But alone and on a bike? Where on earth did you come from?" I was safe—here was a house and somebody who spoke English. My fears vanished and I could not help laughing; the situation seemed too funny now. "Would you like to come in for a cup of tea?'' God Bless the English! It sounded like a formal invitation. All of a sudden I felt weak, and my bike rolled away and crashed into a fence as I sank to the ground. The gentleman, greatly concerned, helped me up and led me into the house. While I recovered in a deep armchair, he put on water for the tea. He left for a while, and when he returned he had changed from his work clothes to the obligatory British shorts and white knee stockings. Now it was my turn to be embarrassed. Covered with sweat and dirt and with my clothes and hair disheveled, I certainly did not look like a presentable lady. Gallantly he offered me his facilities and waited while I took a shower and refreshed myself; then we sat down for the tea party.

It turned out that he was an agronomist, living alone and experimenting with different methods of farming. Since he appeared ill at ease I did not ask why he was living alone far away out in the bush. His terribly formal manners made one feel that he was not used to company and he was probably wondering what to do about this female intrusion into his privacy. Therefore, as soon as I felt strong enough, I thanked him for the tea and asked him to drive me to the mission; I would not dare to go there alone on my bike. He was visibly relieved and brought out his landrover which had room for both me and my bike. Recovering his composure, he offered to drive me close to the bush fire since that was what I had set out to see. Again there were glowing eyes in the dark, but sitting in a landrover beside the man with his rifle, I was not frightened anymore.

We stopped on a hill overlooking the burning plains. The wind which had fanned the flames before had died down and in front of us was a carpet of glowing embers. From time to time our faces were lit up when the flames engulfed a tree or a dry shrub; then we could hear the distant crackling. But the bush fire had obviously spent itself. The agronomist told me the villagers had set the fire to burn the high grass on the plains. This was done not only because of the danger of wild animals hiding in it, but also because lightning would often kindle the dry grass and such a fire could burn out of control. Sweeping fast in the parched bush it could easily destroy villages, and burning quickly along the roads it might trap the people trying to flee. When setting a fire themselves the villagers skillfully used wind and water to guide its direction. They would light the fire on an evening when the wind was weak and when rain might fall to help extinguish it after a while.

As we drove to the mission the Englishman told me about his own battles with fire and with wild animals. He had constantly to cut grass all over his plantation. To keep elephants and buffaloes from devastating his crop, he had to patrol his fields every night, chasing the beasts off and shooting those who persisted in coming back. By the time we arrived at the mission he had warmed up a bit and in a friendly manner invited me to visit him another time. Then he would show me his experimental plantation.

After this frightening experience I did not dare to venture far on my bike for some time. I spent more time in Ifakara where I was completely safe, even at night. I had become a familiar sight to the people and it was heartening to notice how they encouraged me to speak Swahili. I was told that when approaching a hut or people sitting in the yard, it was the custom to call out *"Hodi,"* meaning "May I enter?" Unless the people replied, *"Karibu*—Please come," it would be bad manners and sometimes even dangerous to approach any further. When I passed the huts it happened that women would smilingly call *"Karibu!"* thereby inviting me to stay for a while. I would sit with them in the yard, looking on as they cooked their *ugali*, a porridge made of maize or rice, and watched their small children at the same time. A few chickens and dogs also belonged to the household. The women laughed at my curiosity and let me peep into their huts which were without windows and therefore quite cool even in the midday heat. They had hardly any furniture, only a few straw mats and perhaps a handmade bed in one corner. A small fire glowed in the middle of the floor; often an old grandmother would sit there tending the flames. Every morning when I went to the hospital children, who now were used to me, came running. They laughed and played around, trying to catch my attention. Mothers, on the way to the hospital would reprimand them, requesting that they behave properly.

Usually people were friendly, and I began to feel at ease with them. Not so, however, when encountering Masai tribesmen. They belonged to a nomadic tribe roaming the steppes around Kilimanjaro. To me, they seemed to be a personification of Africa: enigmatic and beautiful. These pastoral people with their large herds of cattle often suffered from bovine tuberculosis and tape worms and would walk hundreds of miles to Ifakara to get the best treatment then available. Tall and slender, the men had a proud bearing and looked at any woman with daring eyes. They had a strange way of walking, as if constantly wading through high grass. They moved along slowly and graciously, raising their heads haughtily and holding their long spears with a firm grip. It was said that a Masai boy was not allowed to marry before he had killed a lion with his spear. The much smaller local people kept out of their way. They disliked and were afraid of the Masai and did not permit them to put up their tents in the villages. The Masai women were never seen unaccompanied by their men. They were very different from the local girls and were heavily laden with copper ornaments. Numerous thin copper rings were added together to make broad bands of metal, tightened around arms, legs and neck. Once in place, these rings could never be taken off again, and used to create a big headache for the technician at the hospital when he had to take chest x-rays of the tuberculosis-affected women. At least one helper had his hands full trying to lift up all the copper rings in such a way that they would not obscure the pictures of the patients' cavernous lungs.

When these proud people came to the out-patient clinic, tension was stirred up among the local patients. Towering above all the others, the Masai never waited his turn but walked right up beside the old nurse and without a word stretched out his hand with the clinic card. At first, only seeing the hand, she called out annoyed—"Await your turn!"—but when the hand did not disappear she looked up and met the challenging eyes of the Masai. "O.K., here is your medicine," she said, lowering her voice to avoid a confrontation. She knew from experience that if a Masai felt insulted or provoked, he would swell like a turkey cock and suddenly tear apart his clothes to expose his male attributes—the Masai gesture of aggression towards women.

When Masai passed under my window in the morning on their trek to the hospital, I could hear the copper bangles of their women clanking with every step, as if they were prisoners walking in chains. Were they not? I often wondered.

4
The First Safari

I had been working in Ifakara for about a month when the first call for medical services outside the hospital reached me. It came from a small outpost a day's journey away from Ifakara. The priest there sent the message through his driver who arrived by landrover to fetch fresh supplies and, if possible, take me back with him. I was keen on adventure and immediately agreed to go, although I had no idea what such services would imply. I arranged for one of the nurses at the hospital to look after my patients during the week that I would be absent so that my research would not be interrupted.

We started out before dawn, and it again struck me how beautiful the early morning hours are in the tropics. It always gave me a joyful feeling—the crispness and fragrance of the air, refreshing like a cool bath—and the memory of this pleasure helped me to endure the heat of the day. The soil on the unpaved road took on a deep red in the first rays of the sun; I could see it glow between the green trees on the mountain slope ahead. When we reached the summit we saw the distant blue mountain range of Iringa rising over the morning mist on the Ulanga plains. The mission we planned to reach by evening was called Merera and was situated at the end of the road in the foothills. The driver told me that the best part of the road had been built by the Germans during the first World War and after they left, the Catholic mission kept the road open and expanded it as new outposts were founded in the region. The forests and plains were thinly populated, but when the road was improved, people came from far away to settle alongside it. In their own interest, the newcomers now helped with the upkeep of the road. I could see recently established villages as we drove along, newly built mudhuts with patches of barely cultivated fields among the trees. We came upon crews of men with spades and hoes working on the road. They jumped aside and greeted us with laughter and cheers from the roadside as we passed them in a cloud of dust.

When a new village reached a certain size, an Asian merchant would move in, building his little *duka* shop at a strategic location alongside the road or in the village square. These East Indians were amazing pioneers; in the middle of nowhere their *duka* would hold an incredible variety of merchandise. Built on to the store were the closed-off living quarters of the large family where mother, grandmother, sisters and daughters attended a large flock of children and ran a traditional Asian household while father, grandfather, uncles and grown-up sons worked in the business. The stranger who happened to pass by would be invited into the *duka* where a youngster served the thirsty traveler a cooling drink. The merchant, friendly and busy, would display some articles and surprise the stranger with all kinds of luxury wares, unexpected that far away from civilization. If the traveler should happen to ask for some goods not in store, the shopowner would be most distressed and the customer would be sure to find them there the next time he came around.

On that first safari we stopped at a *duka* around noon, in the worst heat of the day. While the men were discussing different business matters, a sari-clad lady beckoned me to come with her. She took me to the cool living quarters and with a charming smile invited me to rest upon her own bed.

28

She brought tea and Indian cookies. From the whitewashed walls numerous portraits of family members looked down with dignity. In a corner, framed by flowers, was the large photograph of the Ismaili's beloved Aga Khan. The houses of the *duka* owners that I was to see on my travels through the East-African bush, all looked alike. Sparsely furnished with a few oriental carpets, incense burners, cushions and couches, and perhaps an old fashioned ice-chest, they lacked most commodities. I could not help wondering how the delicate ladies in fine saris preserved their good spirits, living as they did out in the bush, far away from other compatriots and friends, sometimes for years on end. As far as I was able to find out they did not have close ties with the Africans living around them. They employed a few, but seemed to keep that same reserved distance as they displayed towards me, which precludes intimate friendship. I suppose they were satisfied with their self-created culture islands, working incessantly for their large families, looking at the pictures on the walls and thinking about a son studying in London or a daughter well married in India, thanks to the money the parents had saved.

Struggling to keep their business going, the men transported goods from Dar-es-Salaam to the interior. They were their own drivers and mechanics. Whoever got stuck on the road would be assured of help if a *duka* truck happened to pass by. Friendly and polite, the Indian would offer his services, even if it meant a long trip to town for spare parts or hours of sweaty work on the car there on the sun-baked road. In the rainy season, when everybody else had given up driving, the Indian merchants with their old trucks would still make it. Daringly they dashed through swelling rivers and skidded along the muddy roads, miraculously getting through the most impossible sections, providing their *dukas* with goods and their antiquated pumps with gasoline. No one who has traveled in the African bush and endured hardship there can think of these Asian traders without a feeling of appreciation and respect.

Refreshed from our stay at the *duka* we continued our

safari. We were now on the plains, and the driver told me to look out for wild animals. Lions, buffaloes, waterbucks, zebras, antelopes and elephants were abundant in this part of the country. I got a thrill out of watching the white birds walking up and down the backs of the brown buffaloes, peacefully picking flies and other insects off their skin. The huge buffaloes would lift their heads and watch the car as we passed, their broad horns showing clearly against the sky. The waters were crowded with crocodiles and hippopotamuses and I thought of them with a nervous feeling in my stomach as we were ferried across a river. The small float hardly offered room for us to stand beside the car. I searched the murky water as the waves leaped over the edges wetting our feet and I hoped we would not encounter such beasts. Half a dozen men stood at one end and with long poles they pushed the vehicle across. They looked at me with curiosity and exchanged remarks which I could not understand, but from their glances and laughter I guessed that they found me rather funny looking. That was nothing, however, compared to the stir which I caused among the people waiting at the mission when we arrived towards evening.

The mission Father came running out as soon as the landrover stopped. He nervously waved off the open-mouthed gazers and whisked me inside, closing the door firmly behind us. I was astonished at this reception, but he explained that many of the people had never seen a white woman before, and their curiosity might be a bother to me. I assured him that I did not mind the people, but when I was on the way to my new night quarters I understood his concern. It was dark before I went to my hut, but people were still waiting. Most of them were women and young girls. The atmosphere was charged with tension. As I was about to close the door, a young woman put her naked foot in the door. I did not want to hurt her, and stopped. I was immediately surrounded by the women. They talked to me in a flurry of words and laughed because I did not understand. They reached out to touch my hair, they stroked my arms, and before I knew what was happening, they had lifted up my skirt, uttering cries of "oh" and "ah" when they saw I was white all over. I could not help feeling frightened by the intensity of their curiosity when some of them even poked their fingers into my mouth, eyes and ears. Seeing that I did not get angry, people pushed forward and stretched out their hands to touch my body. A scuffle ensued and I used the confusion to slip inside and lock the door. Cries of disappointment and knocks at the door followed, but I did not dare to open again. An instant later the small window openings were packed with dark faces peeping in. I could see the reflection of my lamp in the many staring eyes. The sight gave me an eerie feeling, the like of which I had never experienced before. I felt too uncomfortable to undress, only crept under the mosquito net, blew out the light and lay motionless hoping the people would go away. I do not think they did because when I awakened in the morning a pair of eyes looked at me from the window. I heard a shout, running feet and there they were again, the laughing faces at the windows.

I washed and dressed myself with all kinds of comments from the onlookers. When I began to comb my hair the women outside went into hysterics. They pulled at the door and shouted in unison for me to open it. In daylight their behavior appeared less frightening and since they had apparently never seen long hair before, I opened the door while I continued to comb it. The women looked astounded. Some of them seemed to go into a trance. Glassy-eyed and unaware of what they were doing, they mimicked my every movement. Others, completely perplexed, moved around aimlessly and some turned upside down, literally standing on their heads! Again the vehemence of their emotional agitation scared me and I hurried across the yard and fled into the Father's house followed on my heels by the crowd of enthusiastic women. The Father had to come out and reprimand them. He told them that it was bad *heshima*, disrespectful, to behave so uninhibitedly towards a stranger. They finally calmed down and began to disperse, laughing as they went and discussing what they had seen.

31

After we had eaten and I had recovered from this initial shock, the Father took me to the dispensary, a small building quite some distance from the mission. He showed me his supply of medicines, told me about the most common diseases the people suffered from and introduced me to the patients who had already gathered there. After a while he was called away and I was left alone. Not before that moment had I fully realized what it meant to treat patients of a completely different culture, in a language I could hardly understand and speak even less. During my stay at the hospital there had always been somebody around who helped out. Most people in Ifakara spoke some English or if not, they were used to making themselves understood by Europeans. But here it was a different story and with mounting apprehension I found out how limited my knowledge of their language was. I suddenly felt very alone and frightened in the little dispensary, surrounded as I was by sick people who assumed I could understand their complaints. Suppressing my anxiety I tried to organize my thoughts and actions. I decided to listen quietly to their rapid talk and to say as little as possible so they would not notice how poorly I understood. In the meantime I would use my eyes, hands and stethoscope to examine each patient individually. It did not take me long to recognize that a good part of the people visiting the dispensary that morning were not ill and probably came out of curiosity to see me. People here suffered from malnutrition and anemia and therefore I could give them vitamin and iron pills knowing that they would be helped in some way. During my stay at Ifakara hospital I had learned how to diagnose and treat common tropical diseases, and therefore felt confident that I could detect malaria and other parasitic illnesses even without understanding much of what the patients said.

As the day progressed I began to feel more confident and to pick up more of their language. The moaning of those in pain and the shrieks of frightened children created a sombre atmosphere in the room, but I admired how readily the crowd would respond with laughter to any funny situation. There was a young man who came in with a small abscess on his abdomen. It needed an incision and the man, not knowing exactly what I was up to, calmly lay down and looked on while I prepared for the small operation. But when I approached him with the scalpel, he looked at the knife in my hand for a shocked moment. Then he leaped up and rushed out of the room knocking people aside as he ran. He must have thought that I was going to cut open his belly for he did not return and the room resounded from the laughter of the gleeful women who had watched the scene. Unfortunately such cheerful moments were rare. I was faced with the most horribly infected wounds and broken limbs, situations where I had to use all my courage for the painful manipulations necessary. I could not stop marveling at the patients' endurance of pain, as well as the fantastic healing tendency of their injuries. This type of treatment needed few words and both the patients and I were satisfied with the results.

I began to enjoy my work until one day my anxiety returned when I had to see a patient and simply could not understand what was the matter. The woman was brought to me on a homemade stretcher. The family members who had come along tried to explain what was wrong with her. They appeared unusually tense and upset. The patient sat in a peculiar stiff position on the stretcher holding her head up with both hands. When I wanted to examine her, the people became acutely agitated and the woman cringed at the slightest touch. Her neck and shoulder muscles felt tight like boards. She herself said nothing, only stared out into space. I tried to ask some questions and while listening to the peoples' talk, everything in the book went through my mind, but I could not find any possible diagnosis to fit her condition. Finally I had to send for the Father. He spoke with the excited people and explained to me: "This woman tried to hang herself this morning. Her people cut her down from a tree before she choked to death and brought her here right away." Now I understood; this woman had a broken neck, or at least one that was badly dislocated. I was quite shocked. The possibility of somebody in this wilderness trying to commit suicide had not even crossed my mind. What lay behind this tragedy the people did not tell us. Lacking proper devices, there was no way I could treat her; the slightest change in position of her neck could mean instant death. I had to tell them that I could not cure her out here in the bush; she should be taken to the small Danish mission hospital which was a day's march farther on towards Malinyi. They silently picked her up and went away. I followed the sad little troop with my eyes; the immobile woman sitting cross-legged and erect, carried on the stretcher by four young men. Who knew whether they would reach the hospital in time and whether she could ever recover, even if they succeeded in getting her there.

On the last evening, when the patients had left and I was cleaning up the dispensary, a middleaged man entered. He was unusually formal and polite in the way he greeted me. He wanted some medicine, but for the life of me I could not find out what ailed him. I finally gave up and scribbled a message to the Father asking him to find out and send the man back with the information. For some reason the man seemed reluctant to go to the Father, but when he realized that he could not get anywhere with me, he went. After a while he returned with a note from the Father which read: "This pagan chief has several wives. He is not really ill. He has difficulties sleeping but no real sleep difficulties." I looked at the answer for a while. Was this message supposed to be a riddle? Then it dawned on me that the chief's problem was impotence. The African orderlies working with me at Ifakara hospital had told me that impotence was a major problem, aggravated by anemia among the illness-ridden men in the bush. This man too looked rather thin and worn out. How could I help him? This was not the kind of affliction I had been trained to handle. I searched through the many samples of medicines thrown together into a big box. Then I had a bright idea. Remembering that impotence can be positively influenced by means of suggestion, I grabbed a tube containing Redoxon effervescent tablets which I found in the box. I filled a glass with water and dropped the tablet of Vitamin C into it. Holding the glass with the sparkling water up in front of his eyes I solemnly said *"Dawa ya nguvu!*—Powerful medicine!"* With wide open eyes he watched the large tablet sinking to the bottom and dissolving into a myriad bubbles, as if all the strengthening power was rising to the surface like little spirits. "Here, drink it," I said. He took a step backwards, fear in his eyes. I nodded to encourage him, but he turned ash grey as he watched the *nguvu* spirits continue to pop out of the drink. I held up the glass again. With a tremendous effort he reached out for it. He looked at me firmly, then closed his eyes and drank the brew in one gulp. All those little spirits tickled his throat and nose as they tried to escape. Determined to keep them inside once he had them there, he quickly pressed his lips together and pinched his nostrils tightly with his fingers. When he had to breathe he let go with a big blow. He opened his eyes and smiled. I think he felt stronger already. With a beaming face he took the colorful tube with the wonder drug. I told him to drink a glass of "power medicine" every night before going to bed and gave him other vitamin tablets to take during the day.

Happy and encouraged he thanked me and turned to the door. At that moment another man entered the room and my patient quickly concealed the medicine in his clothes. They greeted each other in a very friendly manner but both appeared slightly embarrassed. Again I understood only a few words of what the newcomer said, but his looks and manners told me that he had come on the same errand. I looked through all the supplies in the dispensary, but there were no more effervescent tablets. I provided him with the usual vitamin pills but this obviously did not satisfy him. He must have watched me and the other man through the window, because he insisted upon getting some "power medicine." Could I not look again? I showed him that there was indeed no more *dawa ya nguvu* in the dispensary. The chief in the meantime had been standing at the door thoughtfully watching what was going on. Slowly he unwrapped the tube of Redoxon tablets I had given him. He counted them carefully, all the round tablets, each of them promising one night of power! He pondered over them for a long while, then separated them into two equal piles and gave one of these to his friend with a sigh. Together the two men left the dispensary. Surely that was a generous gesture by the chief, a true sign of friendship. I felt quite moved.

5

Looking Fear in the Face

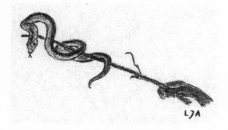

Once having experienced that I could manage on my own, I felt restless in Ifakara. It was quite lonely in the hospital in spite of all the activities there. I also discovered that one of the diseases I was to investigate was rare in the Ifakara region. Writing to several other places and inquiring about this condition, I received a positive reply from Igota, a mission a few hours drive away. The Father wrote that his schoolboys were indeed severely infested with parasites causing that particular disease and he would be grateful for any help I could offer. I could use the laboratory of the mission's dispensary. This would imply helping with the out-patients who were usually cared for by two young dressers trained in Ifakara.

I liked the proposal and discussed it with the nurse who visited there twice a month. She suggested I come along on her next trip. She would introduce me to the patients and let me take over for as long as I intended to stay there. I concluded my research project in Ifakara, and since I planned to be away for at least one month, I took all my belongings. I left Ifakara lightheartedly, not knowing then that apart from a few short visits I was never going to live there again. The research work I had set out to do in Africa was completed within the first year and from then on I became a traveling physician, the *Mama Mganga* who turned up and helped out wherever there was an urgent need for medical services. Once I had started this traveling consultation service, demands steadily increased and before I knew it, I was caught up in the immense task of providing medical services for the large area of the Ulanga district. My stay in Africa turned into a venture lasting much longer than I had planned, and for years I was going to live out of my suitcase. I became used to staying overnight wherever I had a chance, whether I had a bed or not. The mission stations always provided a roof over my head although it sometimes happened that I had to sleep on a mattress in the church or the sacristy where I would again encounter my friends the bats! Sometimes on safaris I slept in the open, protected by a mosquito net fastened to branches and guarded by African scouts. When we heard lions roar in the dark, they would seize their bushknives and look around, assuring me that they knew well how to protect me against any wild animals. The scouts also used to spread ashes from the fire around the legs of my field bed, to prevent ants from crawling up during the night and I always made sure this job was well done for I feared nothing in the bush more than the *siafu*, reddish-brown ants with powerful mandibles which bite fiercely and burrow into the victim's skin.

But I never ceased to love the safaris. They opened up a new dimension of human existence, the long-forgotten life of the nomad which my forefathers had also known when in ancient times they roamed the forests of Northern Europe.

At the small mission where I was to treat the schoolboys I was cordially received and I liked the place right away. My room was large and overlooked the plains. The howling of the hyenas and grunting of the hippos in the nearby river reminded me at night that now I was indeed in the middle of the African bush. Every morning I could hear the chatting and laughing of people waiting outside the dispensary. When I returned from breakfast, the two dressers had already begun their work and had prepared everything for me. Now it was my turn to head an out-patient clinic like the old nurse in Ifakara, examining and treating the sick and ordering tests. I was amazed how much the two young dressers were able to do in their small laboratory. With a microscope, a centrifuge and a few reagents they were able to diagnose the different types of malaria and most parasitic diseases. Patients were usually able to return home after having received their medicine but a few would be kept overnight in a small room adjacent to the dispensary. The seriously ill were taken to Ifakara hospital. My two assistants were easy-going, good-humored young men, thankful for every opportunity to learn and eager to discuss the problems we met with when working together. We were usually able to finish seeing patients in the afternoon. This gave me time for my research project, although I was often interrupted by late arrivals from distant villages.

The school was built on a hill close to the mission. It was an intermediate school for grades five to nine, and those who wanted further education had to go to secondary school at some bigger center. The boys, ranging in age from nine to fifteen, slept in two dormitories, about sixty in each. When I asked for volunteers for my project some hundred eager boys crowded the dispensary. Only forty boys were selected, but even that was more than enough candidates. The headmaster, a local man, accompanied the boys on their first day of treatment. He seemed to be somewhat apprehensive and asked for detailed information about the research and the treatment I intended to give his students. Reserved as he was, there was an air of authority and efficiency about him. I felt rather intimidated by him and could not figure out what he thought of my project. The boys showed great respect for their headmaster and whenever he appeared their otherwise unruly behavior became exemplary.

The illness which I was to investigate and treat was schistosomiasis, one of the most common parasitic diseases of tropical Africa affecting liver, kidneys and bladder. In order to prevent further infestation with the schistosoma parasites, I suggested that all students come to the laboratory for a lecture on prevention. The headmaster arranged for one class at a time to come for the lecture. He himself was present but never made any comment. It was a lecture the boys were not to forget, and it was amusing to observe their reactions when they looked into the microscope. Seeing the enlarged larvae racing around in the drop of urine, some boys jumped from their seats expecting to see these beasts crawling everywhere. Others uttered a cry of fear and did not dare to look again, and some did not dare to look at all. "Witchcraft!" they whispered. It took quite some explanation and persuasion before they overcame their apprehension. I had hoped my demonstration would please the headmaster, but he remained as reserved as before.

Many of the boys would hang around the dispensary all day long. Trying to get my attention with petty complaints and questions, they became a nuisance when I had to treat other patients. Finally we made a deal—if they would leave me alone while I worked, I promised to take time off every afternoon to be with them just for the fun of it. This was readily accepted but hardly respected, and since some of the boys on my project felt sick at times, I could not be too strict with the complainers. We had lots of fun after work, however. I could not help admiring the tireless enthusiasm of these children! They had an insatiable craving for knowledge. Many more boys than the school could accommodate wanted to enrol. I was told that boys who did not make it in the entrance exam cried for days and would persist in trying again. They would hang around the other students and try to learn as much as they could just listening to them. The mission staff always had a group of curious boys on their heels, eagerly observing and picking up anything they could learn. They investigated every car which happened to pass through and built exact car models of bamboo wood and other materials. On the school ground they laid out in an ingenious way a relief map of Tanganyika, constructing roads, bridges, towns, villages, mountains, streams, and now and then adding something new and building on to it. Observing all my moves they offered to do all kinds of services and run errands.

On sports days when villagers came to watch the games the boys would arrange festivities with singing, dancing and drama performances. Playing thieves and police, soldiers and officers in little sketches, they made the school yard resound with the laughter of the onlookers. It was difficult to say who enjoyed it more, the young actors themselves or their audience. They eagerly took up every game I suggested. Especially popular was our shooting competition with bow and arrow. The best marksman of the day received a prize which I had to come up with, and the boys always looked forward to seeing a new trophy. Once I brought a small ice-cube from the mission's fridge. The boys had never seen ice before and at first they dropped it with a cry of "Oh, it burns!" With big eyes they saw the cube disappear as it melted into water in their warm hands. Once they had overcome their fear, this prize became very popular, especially when fruit juice was mixed in.

As my treatment of the schoolboys was nearing its completion, the strain of it began to show. Any remedy aimed at killing parasites acts as a poison at the same time. The toxic substances of the dead and dissolving parasites enter the system and make the patient feel nauseated and generally sick so I monitored each patient carefully and varied the amount of medicine given according to his tolerance. Generally the boys were tolerating the treatment well and I began to breathe easier. Actually I was enjoying myself more than I had since I left Europe. Then suddenly everything began to change into a nightmare.

It started with a frightening experience and a dramatic change in the weather. The long dry season was interrupted by a short rainy period. Every evening for a few days, we saw dark clouds gathering over the mountains. Sheet lightning flashed over the night sky and we heard the rumbling of distant thunder. One day when I opened my medicine chest a green viper disappeared among the bottles. I pulled out my hand with a shriek, and unable to control a sudden panic, I jumped up on the table. People were startled. They must have thought I had gone crazy as I pointed to the cupboard, shouting words they could not understand. Someone ran to fetch the priest and when the people finally understood what was the matter they too became excited. They sent for a famous snake-killer, a man who brought a forked branch sharpened at the ends. Carefully and slowly he made his way between the bottles; I nearly fainted from fear as I watched. The boys later told me I had become as white as chalk. With a quick movement the man pinned the snake in the fork and triumphantly held up the still writhing reptile. It was indeed an extremely poisonous viper. I did not come down from the table until I was sure the snake was dead, and it took me a long time before I got over this shock.

To me the venomous snake seemed like a bad omen and together with the darkening of the sky and the heavy thunder clouds, it gave me an oppressive feeling of anxiety. Something seemed to be wrong with the boys too. In increasing numbers they came to the dispensary complaining of *kichefuchefu,* which meant nausea and headache. They looked worried and said they felt tired and had "pain all over." Suddenly the land showed me a new and threatening face. The clouds grew even more menacing and one evening tore away from the mountains to come upon us with all their vehemence. We could see and hear the tempest approach us: a dark wall of rain and a roar like a waterfall. The wind swept across the dry land; a cataclysm of thunder and lightning broke loose. Everybody ran for shelter and I stood dazed and looked at the drama. But it was not only the weather that frightened me; the condition of the boys burdened my mind and heightened my anxiety. Some of them were seriously ill now. Examining them again I noticed that their livers were enlarged and tender. Many of the boys had fever and abdominal pains. Looking carefully at their eyes I found what I had suspected; the white of the eyes had taken on a yellowish color. There was no doubt the school had been struck by an epidemic of infectious hepatitis. This illness is endemic in the tropics and tends to flare up during

42

changes of the seasons. Malnourished and feeble children are the hardest hit. Thanks to one of the Fathers who was a skillful hunter, the schoolchildren were provided with fresh meat most of the year. The students were therefore well fed and usually such an epidemic would end after a few weeks without any of the students becoming seriously affected. But the boys just recovering from the stressful treatment of their parasitic infestation could not well tolerate another disease on top of it. Their violent reaction frightened the other boys and made them more sick than they would otherwise have been.

Obviously my research work could not be blamed for the epidemic of hepatitis since many other boys were ill as well, but I still felt responsible. I could not help thinking that the headmaster also blamed me for what was happening. Sinister clouds and the flash of lightning surrounded me when I visited the boys in their dormitories. All the joy was gone from their faces. Like broken flowers they hung their heads and pressed their hands against aching stomachs. Over and over again I repeated to myself that it was not my fault, yet I felt shaky and guilty. I had to pull myself together and muster all my courage to call the teachers together for a meeting to discuss what to do. Was there reproach in the eyes of the headmaster? Nobody said anything which could be interpreted as criticism and all listened anxiously to my advice. As long as the boys complained of *kichefuchefu* and showed high temperatures and jaundice, they were to stay in bed. I would come to the dormitories twice a day with medicine and their diet. An adult person would have to stay with them all day, refuse visitors and watch that the patients did not eat anything or get out of bed. If any of the boys became worse I was to be called right away. Since the school had to be closed, the headmaster delegated the teachers to stay with the sick boys. Everybody went around in a gloomy, depressed and anxious mood.

In the days that followed I was barely able to work at the dispensary. My thoughts were constantly with the sick boys. Twice a day I went over to the school, distributing sugar-water and reconstituted milk with vitamins. It had been raining for days and with the rain came cool temperatures and gusty winds. The boys were shivering with cold and fever. Seeing the long rows of boys lying on their beds, wrapped up tightly in grey woolen blankets which also covered their heads, I thought with a shudder that they looked like corpses already. It was like a nightmare and I went around as if in a bad dream, startled out of it from time to time by the glaring lightning and the ear-splitting thunder which drowned the moaning of the sick. Never had I experienced such terrifying thunderstorms. Once I counted more than sixty flashes of lightning in one minute. People walking barefoot through rain and mud became afflicted with sores and wounds; they suffered from colds and coughs and many of them, especially small children, quickly developed pneumonia. Our facilities were overcrowded with patients and there was more work to do than ever before.

Even as the boys began to recover, I could not relax. Somehow I had lost my self-confidence. I caught myself trying to avoid the headmaster. He seemed to personify my feelings of guilt and inadequacy. I believed I could see disapproval and hostility on his face. The boys too had difficulties regaining their good spirits. Clinging anxiously to me as if I was their mother, they regressed to the behavior of small helpless children. They appeared particularly fearful at night and whispered into my ear about evil spirits haunting the dormitories in the dark. I did not understand them well, but when I asked the teachers about it they looked aside without answering and seemed scared themselves. Had the boys become emotionally disturbed? Another reason for anxiety. On Sunday at church I wanted to speak to the priest about my fears, but noticing that the headmaster had approached us and was overhearing what I said, I felt embarrassed and changed the topic.

That evening as I was sitting alone in my room tired and utterly discouraged, there was a knock at the door. A boy brought me a letter from the headmaster. My heart began to beat faster and I hesitated to open it. In my insecure state of mind I feared some sort of reproach; perhaps a suggestion that I had better leave for good. Finally I opened the letter with shaky hands and read:

Dear Doctor, Madam, you are so busy! I am extremely glad that you are so busy, not because I would like you to get tired, but because you are becoming so useful to us and humanity. I believe your profession is akin to mine in the sense that one has to offer one's heart for human-kind. And the joy one gets out of them is too deep and sublime to be experienced by traders and the like, so carry on with brave heart.

But what did you say, Doctor? You are afraid! What are you afraid of? Is the fright in your heart due to some strong tender feelings for your patients or something else? I am sure you know what you are afraid of. Understanding the fear and its cause, only one thing remains for a brave person as you are, that is to fear that fear itself. I hope it will not take long before you are able to conquer the fear, if you practise to fear the fear. Be all courage and no fear! Lo! You are doing a lot for Africa and Africans. Why are you so anxious? Keep up your head, Doctor! I know that advices are more simply said than followed, but this does not render them being said useless. Excuse me for writing this letter. I wanted you to know that you are not alone and that I am your friend.

For a long while I sat quietly. The sincere and touching words of the headmaster were balsam to my troubled mind. I read the letter again. It was shocking to realize how I had misjudged this man. I had projected my own feelings about myself onto him, seeing him as an unfriendly person quite different from what he really was like. Could it be that nobody blamed me for what had happened? As I sat there with the heartwarming letter in my hands I began to relax. A heavy load was lifted from my shoulders. The boys were on the way to recovery, there was no reason to be anxious any more. The headmaster was right. I should fear my own fear, the tendency I had of becoming intimidated and anxious when things did not turn out the way I wanted. "Be all courage and no fear," the headmaster wrote. Maybe that is what courage is all about: to face threatening events, do what is humanly possible and not allow oneself to be overcome by fear when things take a bad turn. The headmaster seemed to know. He also showed me that in difficult times friendship is essential and that if one feels lonely it is due to self-imposed isolation. The next day when I saw the headmaster at the school, I went up to him and thanked him for his letter. He smiled and said, "Well doctor, the boys are getting better. Soon we can start the classes and then I will look after the boys myself."

In the evening somebody knocked at my door again. This time it was the headmaster himself. He had brought his guitar and one of the younger teachers. They were wondering if I would like some entertainment. Since there was only one chair in my room they had to sit on my bed. They looked at each other and grinned while the headmaster fumbled nervously with the strings. With shaky voices they tried out a few melodies but were continuously interrupted by their own giggles and laughter. I thought they were exceedingly charming and was again amazed how I could have misjudged the headmaster so badly. Finally the two teachers cleared their throats and began to sing. Their gentle voices blended beautifully with the delicate tones of the guitar. I had to hold back my tears; it was rare that anybody thought of cheering me up. My enthusiasm encouraged them and their songs sounded livelier. Before they left, a warm feeling of friendship had sprung up between us and I asked them please to come again another evening. They did, although sometimes after a day's work at the school they were obviously very tired, especially the younger teacher, who often could not keep his eyes open. He inevitably fell asleep upon my bed. The headmaster would continue to play for a while and then start to talk. He told me about his life when he was growing up in a small village. I believe it was the first time that he had spoken so openly to a European. Noticing my interest in traditional African medicine, he revealed to me that his grandfather was a medicine man and that he was taught in this art because the old man had hoped his grandson would take over from him. But he had been too afraid of the powerful spirits of his grandfather and decided to leave home, convert to Christianity and train as a school teacher. He could never forget what he had learned from his shaman grandfather, however. He had experienced the supernatural power of the old people and seen how this power was used or misused.

Every time his friend fell asleep on the bed, the headmaster would tell me more of the secret lore. He talked about poison which medicine men could make move by itself. The poison would slowly creep forward on the ground and "sniff out" its victim, enter him unnoticed and make him sick. "Do you know about the *zombi*?" the headmaster once asked, lowering his voice so as not to awaken his friend. As I indicated my ignorance, he looked at me searchingly, as if to assure himself I did not laugh at what he was telling me. I felt uncanny under his piercing glance. "Well," he began, "some medicine men specialize in black magic. We call such a person a *mchawi*, a wizard. My grandfather who was a *mganga*, medicine man, had to know something about their sorcery to be able to fight it. He told me that when a *mchawi* wants a helper to carry out his evil deeds, he secretly chooses a certain young man and poisons him. The poison makes the young man fall into a deep sleep. He becomes completely rigid so that his family thinks he is dead and buries him. In the night after the funeral the *mchawi* sneaks to the grave and digs out the man. He carries him to a secret hut somewhere in the bush. While the man is still in his death-like sleep the *mchawi* cuts out his tongue so that the man will never be able to speak again. Even when the poor man wakes up from his sleep the *mchawi* keeps him in a trance state. The mute man, now a *zombi*, is completely under the influence of his master, a submissive slave who will carry out any order the *mchawi* gives him. In a trance state, he is sent out at night on sinister errands of evil. He will blow poison into the huts of hapless victims or pour lethal medicine into their food or even crawl into their huts and put it into a sleeping person. People are deadly afraid of the *zombi.* Having already died, he cannot be killed by ordinary people. There are no ways they can harm him and their only protection is the medicine man or another *mchawi* whose power is greater. The *zombi* is doomed if he shows any sign of disobedience or tries to get in contact with his family. His master will let him die completely." The headmaster ended his gruesome account and we both fell silent. "You know," he continued after a while, "that's why the boys have been so frightened at night. They have seen a *zombi* in the dark, heard him stalking around outside, seen his dead-man's hand at the window, a shadow sneaking along the walls. Somebody wanted to harm them. It was the *zombi* who caused the illness they have been suffering from." I thought of the howling wind at night, the sound of branches being thrown around, the hammering of raindrops on the roof and the scary thunderstorms. It was not difficult to imagine how the culture-bound concept of the *zombi* could conjure up threatening fantasies in the terrified children. I did not dare ask whether the headmaster also believed in the *zombi*'s reality.

Fortunately for us all, the weather cleared and when the sun was shining warmly during the day and the moon brightened up the night, the thoughts of spooks disappeared. The boys, recovered from their illness, took up school work as eagerly as ever before and when I had to leave for other tasks the mission was again resounding with their happy laughter. Long after I had left this mission I received the sweetest letters from boys I had treated:

> Dear *Mama Mganga,* I am very sorry to write this letter because I have no aim; so it is better to excuse me. Thank you for having treated me so well, but I am very, very angry just because you leave me alone for a long time. This is why I am very sad. I love you very much and now I do not know what I shall do with my loveness to you. Yours thankfully, Theodos.

> Hullow dear doctor. I am your friend now, and the

word 'Friend' means one who has kindly feelings towards one another, or a person whom one likes very much. Remember me doctor, I am not going to forget you until I die; remember me, remember me, send me only one book or two for medicine, I want to study them, I shall do the work which you do now. Your photo, I want to see it as quickly as you can. Goodbye my friend, yours faithfully, Ali.

One of the boys had asked to borrow my bicycle so he could visit his sick father in Ifakara. Sometime later I received the following letter:

Dear mother, I can start forwarding nothing than wishing to know about your present physique. Are you well? As regards to me I am still well together with my fat stomach and means of what I possess. The bicycle is all right, but it is somehow not in good order because the sponge of the saddle is not in good order and also one of the rubber of front brakes is off and lastly the cover of the valve of the front wheel went off while I was riding. But I have replaced a blue cover instead. I am very grateful because you borrowed me your bicycle; you may tell me anything which you would like me to do, or if at all you need a help from me. Please forgive me for bad English and wasting your time. Yours truly, Samuel.

Whenever I returned to the mission, the schoolboys would come running and greet me jubilantly, jumping around in sheer excitement. They flocked around me, grasping my hands and touching me, all wanting to talk at the same time. But none of the boys who had written letters revealed themselves to me in person. I guess they feared the teasing of the other boys.

6

Dresser Ndogo's Tragic End

The so-called "dressers" of the medical service in Tanganyika were typical products of the colonial system. Not given enough training to be medical doctors, but having learned more about the use of medicines than the nurses, they were equipped for the purpose of helping doctors in rural areas. In colonial times medical doctors were mostly non-Africans and since there were never enough doctors to fill the needs of the medical centers, dressers often found themselves having to take responsibility far above the level they had been trained for. There they were, these young African men, working alone in small, badly equipped dispensaries out in the bush. Always in dire want of essential equipment, with only limited drug supplies and without a hospital within reach to send patients to, they had to treat even the most gravely ill patients and therefore worked under severe stress.

I greatly admired the dressers who worked for months on end without outside help, always watched with suspicion by their desperate clientele lest they keep the best medicines for their own family and friends and readily accused of malicious intent and witchcraft when treatment failed or patients died.

Their workday never ended; day and night their services were in demand. Few dared to take time off for their private lives, sometimes not even for sleep. Now and then a medical doctor or some government health inspector would bring in new supplies and stay for a while. The dressers would view these inspections with mixed feelings. Knowing little about the daily toil of the men in the field, the foreign doctor might criticize any lack of hygiene and orderliness in the dispensary; not familiar with the fact that few instruments and insufficient remedies were available, he would often make useless recommendations which the dresser was too polite to dispute, but had to discard for practical reasons. This would leave the dresser frustrated and insecure. Dressers working for the mission had an easier life. The Fathers would help them and back them up in difficult situations. The missions were also better equipped due to the many donations from physicians in Europe. Sensing the dresser's guarded feelings when I arrived at the scene, I used to think it over carefully before I suggested any changes to improve his work habits or treatment methods. The dresser was the insider who had accumulated experience and knowledge about the diseases common in his area and the best way of treating them with the few medicines available. I, as the physician, was the outsider who came with new ideas but with little knowledge of the complicated situations which develop when demand is greater than supply. Again and again I wondered how these anonymous heroes kept their spirits high. They always seemed to be ready to laugh and joke in spite of their hardships.

Dresser Ndogo was not like the others. He hardly ever smiled and his somber expression made me feel uneasy in his presence. I also noticed that his patients were afraid of him. But he seemed to know how to handle them and he kept his dispensary clean and in good order. Dresser Ndogo was a puny little man in his mid-twenties. He suffered from ill health and his big eyes had the air-hungry expression of an asthmatic. The first time I came into his crowded dispensary he stepped aside without a word and simply made me take over. I could hear his heavy wheezing as he stood there, looking with apparent interest at the way I worked. Having become used to his silence, I was startled when he finally spoke. There was something indefinable in his low, halting voice, but his questions were intelligent and much to the point.

There was something about him that made one hesitate to ask personal questions, but the Father in charge of the mission station told me that dresser Ndogo had suffered from asthma since he was a boy. At the mission school he was an exceptionally bright pupil and the Father had taken a special interest in him. Since both parents seemed to dislike their sickly son, the boy came to look upon the priest as his fatherly friend. The Father remembered how the boy had tried hard to please his parents, and that the mother had been especially rejecting, causing the boy much sorrow. The situation improved some when the boy earned money and sent her regular monthly payments. Soon after the boy had finished his training as a dresser, the Father was transferred to another outpost. But no dresser wanted to work there because the Wangindo tribesmen were known for their use of witchcraft and poisons. Not only did they employ cardiac toxins to kill game, their medicine men were renowned for their knowledge of all kinds of poisonous decoctions. It was said that they knew ways of making a person go insane, or of causing internal bleeding or other afflictions which would slowly kill the victim. Dresser Ndogo had been very upset when hearing that his friend the Father had to work among the Wangindo people and one day he turned up to share life at the remote mission station with him. Dresser Ndogo lived in a small hut by himself and nobody knew what he did in his spare time. He hardly made any friends and rarely ventured out among the people. But since he was a conscientious dresser who knew his trade well, people flocked to his dispensary and, although he was a stranger, he commanded a certain prestige among the tribesmen.

In the days that followed I found out that it was interesting to work with dresser Ndogo. In contrast to most of the others, he stayed with me the whole time when I treated

52

patients. In his quiet way, he made me aware of many things I had not yet been able to pick up due to my scanty understanding of the language and customs, and he even allowed himself to smile at my blunders. I remember once getting angry with a young mother for bringing her sick infant in in a deplorably neglected condition. "Your child will die if you don't take better care of it," I said. A commotion arose among the patients, and the young mother picked up her baby and left without letting me touch it. Later dresser Ndogo explained, "You must never say to a mother that her child will die. People can't understand your reasons for saying that. They think you want to punish the mother and that instead of curing the child you will kill it."

Dresser Ndogo accompanied me every time I was asked to visit patients in their huts, even when it meant marching for hours through the bush after work. On these trips he hardly spoke a word and I could never figure out whether he came along of his own free will or because the Father requested it. His silence was probably due to his asthma which made it hard for him to keep up with me, but whenever I stopped to let him get his breath or offered to treat his asthma he turned hostile and sullen. One morning, however, I found him suffering from such a severe attack that he could neither move nor speak. I quickly prepared an injection and without first asking, gave him the shot. The prompt relief from the spasm that followed surprised him greatly and from then on he gratefully accepted my treatment. Gradually we developed a kind of friendship based upon respect and the task we had in common. Sometimes on our long journeys, especially if we were alone and his asthma did not bother him too much, he would ask questions about the world outside. He was greatly interested to hear how patients in Europe were treated. I remember he was very amused when I told him that asthma was not uncommon among white people.

In the region where we traveled I noticed that people appeared exceptionally scared when meeting me in the bush. Mothers would pick up their terrified children, two or three at a time, and dash off into the thicket yelling "*Wachinji-chinji.*" When I asked dresser Ndogo what this meant, he became very embarrassed and it took a long time before he would explain: "People in this remote area have only vague ideas about the rest of the world. A few of them have been to a hospital. They return with weird stories about white people keeping human blood in glass bottles. Having had blood samples drawn for laboratory testing, they imagine that the whites use their blood for all kinds of sinister purposes. They believe that the 'European birds,' the airplanes, can only fly when given human blood as fuel. Fantastic stories are circulated about how the whites get the blood they need. People say African children in the bush are lured by Europeans with gifts; they are caught, blindfolded, strung up on trees, their bloodvessels opened and the blood collected in glass bottles. *Chinja* means 'cutting the throat—slaughter.'" I was quite shocked. How then did the sick dare to take my treatment and swallow my medicines? "The more dangerous a doctor the more effective his remedies." explained Ndogo, the dresser.

Several months had passed when I was again asked to stay for a while at the same remote mission. I found dresser Ndogo looking more sinister than ever. In some ways he had changed and appeared suspicious and depressed. When he laughed, which I had not heard him do before, it sounded uncanny and cold. A heavy wheezing indicated that his asthma was getting worse. The Father told me that dresser Ndogo had planned to buy a bike so he could travel home for a visit. Since he wanted to go before the rainy season set in and made the road impassable, he had to save up his money quickly and had therefore neglected to send the usual amount home to his mother. One day an angry letter from her arrived which made him extremely upset. He carried the letter around not knowing what to do and finally showed it to the Father. "It would have been better if you had never been born," wrote his mother, and dresser Ndogo shed many tears over that.

Around this time a young girl who had fallen in love with dresser Ndogo used to hang around the dispensary. Feeling more lonely and rejected than ever, he had finally invited her to come to him one evening but had apparently been unable to make love to her. This was considered a great disgrace for a young woman and the girl had left him in anger. Dresser Ndogo now began to feel people were laughing at him behind his back. He believed he heard somebody call him "the child," which painfully indicated to him that his mishap was being talked about. He lost his usual grip on the patients and withdrew more than ever into solitude, hardly eating anything for fear that the food might be poisoned by the girl's family as an act of revenge. I felt very sorry for him and tried to boost his shattered pride by praising him and asking for his advice in front of the patients. This seemed to help and soon dresser Ndogo was almost his old self again.

On our trips through the bush, friendly people often offered us a drink of *pombe*. This nutritious home-brewed beer, made out of fermented rice, is contamination safe because of its alcohol content. Since one cannot drink untreated water in the tropics I was always happy to accept this refreshing drink. One day when passing a compound of huts we were invited in for the usual drink. Dresser Ndogo had just emptied his bowl and I stretched out my hands to receive mine when suddenly an old man snatched the bowl from me, took a sip and then politely returned it to me. From a dark corner rang the laugh of a young girl. Looking at her, dresser Ndogo turned ash gray. Gasping for breath and with a wild look in his eyes, he dashed out of the hut and ran down the path. Very much alarmed I followed him as quickly as I could. It was already getting dark when I nearly stumbled over his crouching body as I hurried towards the mission. He seemed to be scared out of his mind and was wheezing and struggling for air. It took a long time to make sense out of his mumbling. "I am lost! They finally got me! I am dying, there was poison in the *pombe*." Cold fear gripped me but for his sake I tried to suppress it. I shook his shoulder, "Listen, I drank from the *pombe* too and I don't feel anything." Dresser Ndogo wrung his hands. "No, no," he moaned between his gasps. Had I not noticed how the old man drank from the beer first before offering it to me? This was the custom to demonstrate to guests that the drink was not poisoned. But nobody had tasted the drink they gave to *him*! He became aware of it when he noticed the girl in the corner. That girl wished him no good and now he was going to die. His eyes widened with fear and he trembled all over. I tried in vain to calm him down. We had both drunk from the same source, I said, and the old man would not have taken a sip of the brew had it been poisoned. But dresser Ndogo was inconsolable. His teeth chattered as he explained: "I have been told these people have a very strong poison which they can conceal under the thumb nail. Filling the bowl to the very brim when handing the drink to the person they want to kill, they inconspicuously dip the thumb into the brew. By drinking first, the old man wanted to show that he was not out to harm *Mama Mganga,* only the man who had disgraced his daughter."

Dresser Ndogo was beside himself but I had to find a way to get him home. Making myself appear angry I said that was enough of this nonsense. It was all no more true than the *wachinji-chinji* stories; he should feel ashamed to let himself be scared like this. We were doctors ourselves and would show these people who had the stronger medicine. If he did not pull himself together, the asthma would kill him, if nothing else. I finally got him up and holding on to each other, we slowly proceeded through the dark. We were both badly shaken. My heart was pounding and besides fearing that a leopard or other wild animal would leap at us from the dark, I seemed to see strange shadows of witch-doctors lurking behind the trees. As soon as we reached the mission we woke up the Father and told him the whole story. He too tried in vain to calm the dresser, but nothing could take away dresser Ndogo's conviction that he was doomed. I finally gave him a sedative and we asked a mission teacher to stay with him through the night.

The next morning dresser Ndogo did not appear for work and fearing the worst the Father and I hurried down to his place. We found him standing in the middle of the room, holding on to the teacher with all his might. "He won't let go of me," said the embarrassed teacher. "He won't let go of me," repeated dresser Ndogo in a high-pitched voice. "What's the matter with you?" asked the Father. "What's the matter with you?" echoed the dresser. Whatever we said, he repeated it; whenever we made a gesture, he did the same. He seemed scared out of his wits, and as a bronchial spasm nearly choked him in his agitated state and did not disappear even with medication, we decided that he had to be taken to Ifakara hospital some hundred miles away. The teacher and the Father would go with him while I stayed to treat the patients who already waited at the dispensary. Just before the car left, dresser Ndogo came to his senses. He hung his head sadly and muttered, "You too want to get rid of me—I know you are sending me away, but I have done no wrong. Please don't leave me alone." For a moment I hesitated. I thought it was better for him to leave this place for many reasons; he looked too sick, and I did not dare to treat him at this outpost. He turned away with a hurt but also suspicious look in his eyes, and I knew he felt rejected again.

In the days that followed I found it hard to keep my mind on the daily work at the dispensary. Everybody around me was upset and was discussing endlessly what had happened to dresser Ndogo. I could not understand much of what people said, but I could sense apprehension and fear in their behavior and agitated talk. On his return the Father reported that dresser Ndogo had been quiet during the long journey to the hospital. When people asked him where he was going, he replied passively, "I don't know where they are taking me." But when he was handed over to the hospital staff, dresser Ndogo reacted with panic. He pushed aside doctor and nurses and ran through the corridors, fighting off anybody who tried to restrain him. He cried and shouted at invisible enemies until the whole hospital was in an uproar. There are few things the people feared more than a mentally deranged person. It was not physical violence but mysterious powers they were afraid of. Believing that the evil spirits which possessed dresser

Ndogo could be dangerous for others, visitors started to leave the hospital, carrying away their sick relatives. The commotion was such that the hospital administration refused to admit and treat dresser Ndogo. His relatives were called in, and knowing that mentally deranged patients could be sent to the mental hospital, a fate which the Africans dreaded more than death, they decided to take dresser Ndogo home with them. They skilfully subdued the raving man, swiftly tying his hands and feet to a pole which they placed along his back. To avoid chafing the skin they placed cloth under the ropes. Feeling that he was immobilized, dresser Ndogo gave up the fight and again passively endured whatever happened. The relatives lifted him up by the pole, placed him upon a simple stretcher and carried him off to his brother's place, far away from the hospital. "Who knows what will happen to our friend now," the Father ended his sad report.

When the first chance turned up to visit the area of dresser Ndogo's brother, I lost no time in hiring a local villager to take me to the brother's place, hoping that I could be of some help to my unfortunate friend. The guide told me that dresser Ndogo had become increasingly disturbed. Following traditional custom his brother had consulted a local medicine man who was to find out what caused the affliction and treat it. The medicine man had listened to dresser Ndogo's suspicion of having been poisoned, performed all sorts of incantations, and burned certain plants in front of the sick man. According to the notion that ears, nose, eyes and mouth open directly to the brain, the medicine man had blown incense smoke into dresser Ndogo's nostrils and ears. However, to the family's sorrow, he had voiced little hope for the patient's recovery. Yet dresser Ndogo seemed to improve after the medicine man's treatment, until his own father turned up. As soon as dresser Ndogo saw his father, he became acutely disturbed again so that he had to be restrained. Once more, they had called for the medicine man.

I found dresser Ndogo gasping for air in one of his severe asthma attacks. He stood in the yard, hands folded behind his head so as to expand his chest, fear in his eyes. His neck was placed in the fork of a thick branched pole, held there by a cloth bound around the ends. The lower end of the pole was tied to a rope which was again fastened around a tree, allowing the patient to move around but not to run away. His hands were loosely tied together over the pole so that he could not touch his body. This clever device prevented him from harming himself, but still left him enough freedom to use his hands above the pole. Dresser Ndogo looked at me and whispered between gasps for air, "Please help me." The brother stood by with some other relatives, not knowing what to do. Deep sorrow marked his face. With one single shot of an antiasthmatic medicine, I was able to relieve the patient's agony. Dresser Ndogo sank to the ground. He dropped his head and tears trickled down his cheeks. "I'm coming with good wishes from the Father," I tried to cheer him up. "He says you should hurry up to get well, he needs your help with all the patients." There was a flicker of a smile. "And you and I, we will start to work with the microscope together," I went on, remembering that he had wanted to learn more about lab techniques. He smiled again and hope seemed to light up his sad face. But his eyes wandered around suspiciously. Suddenly he grasped my arm. "Do you see that old man?" He pointed at his father who crouched by the hut. "He is not my father, he is an evil spirit." Hearing this the poor old man withdrew further into the shadow. Dresser Ndogo pulled me closer. "He wants to kill me," he whispered with desperation in his voice. I tried to reassure him and promised to visit him daily. But dresser Ndogo stared out into the air as if listening. Again fear was reflected in his face. "Don't you hear the water coming?" he murmered. "The lions roar, the drums are sounding. I cannot go home—the church bells are announcing my end." He closed his eyes and seemed to fall asleep. His father made a move. Dresser Ndogo jumped up. "Stay away!—don't move!—don't kill me!" he yelled, and ran as far as the pole and the rope allowed. His brother and another man subdued him, untied him and carried him inside the hut.

Gently they placed him on a bed. Whilst talking to him in a soothing friendly voice they secured him tightly to the bed. Apologetically they assured me that the sick man would always calm down when restrained so that he could not move at all. Dresser Ndogo looked at me with wide open eyes. "You see what they are doing to me?" he said with a somber, hostile expression. No reassuring or kind word seemed to reach his frozen mind. When the sedative I gave him took effect, he fell into a deep sleep, sweat pearling on his forehead. I left in a downcast mood, but with the impression that the relatives really cared for dresser Ndogo.

During the following days it became obvious that dresser Ndogo would not survive. He refused to eat, thinking that all food was poisoned. We persuaded his father to leave since the patient seemed to fear him the most. But as soon as the sick man found his father had left, his anxiety intensified and we had to recall the old man. Dresser Ndogo now insisted upon having his father close at his side so that he could watch him all the time and prevent him from doing evil. When asthma attacks were choking him, dresser Ndogo had lucid moments, but when they eased off he became increasingly confused and hallucinated, until his mounting anxiety again triggered off another severe asthma attack. At times he would hold my hand and calm down, but mostly he did not seem to recognize anybody except for his father whom he watched with suspicion.

The end came after one of his exhausting asthma attacks. He died quietly, like a flame slowly going out for lack of air. It was just before the rainy season, during the week in which he had planned to travel home on his new bicycle to visit his mother.

The Children of Ngombe

The dry season was nearing its end. On the slope of the Mahenge mountains where the Ruaha mission stood, the thick tropical forest held enough moisture to keep the trees and plants lush and green. But on the plains below, the leaves were withered and the grass turned brown. Fire swept through the dry grass, blackening the bush and leaving the plain naked and even drier than before. Frightened by the smoke and uncomfortable without the shelter of the thick bush and high grass, the wild animals roamed restlessly over wide areas, gathering towards the evenings at the few remaining water holes. There small, floating plants covered the surface and helped to conserve the dwindling water. The ponds were teeming with life; frogs croaked among the leaves and thousands of insects were humming over the green carpet, while lions and hyenas waited for their thirsty prey in the bushes at the edges. Now and then the motionless surface was disrupted by a snorting head of a hippopotamus; it seemed to warn of the many dangers lurking in the deep below.

The people living on the plain were hard put for water themselves, but feared the supernatural power they thought

61

was hovering over the water holes. They preferred the foul-smelling liquid they could still draw from their own wells but they suffered from thirst and dirt. During this time an increasing number of sick people came to the mission of Ruaha and the Fathers asked for my help.

Upon my arrival at the mission, a big crowd of small children gathered around our landrover. They clung to each other like a frightened herd of deer and looked at me with alarm and curiosity. I learned that they were children from the far-off village of Ngombe. With their teacher, they had come to the mission to ask for the treatment of bilharzia, a parasitic disease from which they all suffered. Children playing around in the murky waters are especially prone to contract this disease, for larvae of the bilharzia parasite penetrate the skin of those who wade into the water. They lodge in the wall of the bladder and cause pain and considerable blood loss. I looked at the crowd of thin and undernourished children and hesitated to take them on. They seemed such a bunch of wild kids and they spoke a language quite different from the Swahili I knew. The treatment would strain them and would last for a week. How would I be able to keep track of these unruly children besides all the other work I had to do? Noting my hesitation the teacher shouted something and the children ran off into the bush. I could hear them whimper while they were urinating. Soon they returned with tears of pain still on their cheeks, and with thin arms each held up a bottle, showing me the blood-stained urine. How could I send them back to their village as sick as they were? The mission offered full cooperation and was to provide food and lodging. The teacher would act as guard and interpreter and help me with the children. Finally, with much worry I consented to treat the children.

The first day of treatment was a nightmare. Everything at the mission station was new and frightening to these children of the wilderness and they were already pretty scared when they lined up for their first injection. The children's eyes widened as they watched me prepare the syringes. It took the teacher much persuasion before the first child dared to bend down for the needle. The scream of pain which followed nearly scared the others out of their wits. But since they wanted to get well, they mustered all their courage and most of them went through with the treatment. In the evening I went over to their quarters. I thought it would be best to get acquainted with them in a more pleasant way and hoped they would then have less fear. At first they were quite timid, but gradually curiosity took over and they came close. Cautiously they began to touch me. They burst out laughing when I wiggled my white toes in my sandals; they wanted to know whether I was white *all over* my body. When dusk fell and we had eaten a simple meal together, they became more confident and some started to sing. When they saw that it pleased me, the others soon joined in. A strangely beautiful scene: the small flame of the lamp flickering under their breath was reflected in the eager, lively eyes of the children and made their teeth shine as they opened their mouth and sang with all their might.

The following afternoon the children smiled when they saw me, and the whole procedure went much faster. The funny little rascals! Those who had already gone through the ordeal would gather beside me and look with glee at the others still standing in line. With mounting anxiety the waiting children would step from one foot to the other. Some cried out, "Mama wee..." while others whistled to get rid of the tension, but when their turn came they all courageously bared their behinds. Everybody was laughing heartily when the poor kids hopped around crying and pressing their hands on the place of the injection.

On the fourth day the urine was clear, but the children felt sick and weary. The medicine caused them to vomit. The teacher comforted the children as much as he could since I was too busy with other patients to give them much attention during the day. When I visited them in the evening, there were no happy singing children any more. They sat around hanging their heads and only wanted to lie down. I felt worried and decided to let them have a day of rest before they received their last shot. The teacher was instructed to give them plenty to drink and to keep them out of the sun on the following day.

That day was exceptionally hot and I was too busy at the dispensary to inquire about the children. It was nearly evening when I finally hurried to see them. Their quarters were empty; the children were gone. I learned that the poor little ones had felt sick and wanted their mothers, so they had sneaked away in the middle of the day and run home. I was startled to hear that the teacher had gone along without contacting me first; he had obviously not realized how sick the children were. My uneasiness about the whole undertaking had been only too well-founded. A feeling of impending disaster was weighing me down. I could visualize the children, weakened from their illness and from the incomplete treatment, running through the bush in the scorching sun, without food and water for hours. More than fifty little children—and only one irresponsible adult to take care of them. What would happen? What could I do? The food dried up in my mouth at the dinner table. "Everything is in God's hands," said one of the Fathers, who saw my distress. I looked at him with dismay. That was no comfort for me now. Quick steps approached from outside. Somebody asked for me. All blood drained from my face; the first catastrophic news had arrived. One little girl had collapsed and died shortly after she reached the hut of her parents. The other children were scared and exhausted as they lay around prostrated in the village, said the messenger. Night was falling. There was nothing I could do.

Early next morning Father Superior arrived at my door with the deserted teacher. Their faces were somber. Another girl had died during the night and the people in the village were upset and frightened. They were convinced that all the children would die. Rumors had it that I was a witch who wanted dead children for some sinister purpose. My heart pounded and my knees started to tremble. "I must go to the village right away." Father Superior looked at me. "It could be dangerous." "But I have to go. I must treat the children or more of them will die," I exclaimed. Nobody could argue this point. The Father reluctantly agreed to take me there. Hastily medical supplies and other equipment for a week's stay in the bush were packed and sent off with porters, and soon we were riding on a motorbike towards the village. There was no time to think about the situation or what was awaiting me.

The narrow path through the bush was rough and at times perilous. It must have taken the children half a day to reach their homes. The sun was already burning when we approached the first huts and there a group of people blocked our way. News of our arrival had reached Ngombe, but I don't know how, since we had come much faster by motorbike than any man could run. The people were the village elders who wanted to know what I was up to. We had to sit down with them and explain carefully all that had happened. The teacher, for obvious reasons, had kept quiet about the children's running away before the treatment had been completed. I had come here to finish it. The village elders talked among themselves and then invited us to follow them to one of the huts. In there was one of my patients, "half dead," as they said. They wanted to see what I could do for him. Fortunately the little boy was not seriously ill, only exhausted and weak from lack of food and water. I hastily prepared some sugar-water, a remedy I had on many occasions found helpful for half-starved people in the bush. Soon the child felt better, and as everybody could see how he was recovering, we were allowed to proceed.

Close by the small school house on a parched meadow stood a half-crumbled mud hut. That was to be my quarters. The Father unloaded my things. He asked me to send one of the porters who were to arrive with my equipment to the mission whenever I wanted to be taken back there. Before I could say anything further he mounted his bike and drove off. The dry sound of the motor echoed over the plains, fading away in the distance, and soon the hot air shimmered over the grass as before. Life in the bush is tough; there is little time for sentiments. I felt kind of lost for a while, standing there alone among these strange and suspicious people, who now stared at me in silent curiosity. With a sigh I followed them into the village. They took me to an open place with a cluster of grass-thatched huts. I could hear *kilio,* a sing-song used when mourning the dead. The elders were taking me to the place where the girl had died during the night. I went in, hoping that this child would also be only "half dead." There she was, lying on a mat on the floor, her fragile arms and legs stretched out, her sweet face turned upward. Her eyes were closed and there was a little froth at her mouth. Alas, her limbs were stiff and there was no warmth left in the once so lively body. I gazed at her, numbed with grief. There was silence in the hut. "I am sorry—there is nothing I can do." As I stepped out into the light, a wild party burst forth from the bush. Disheveled women, howling and yelling, their faces painted white, poured handfuls of dirt over their heads. They threw themselves backwards on the ground, rolled around, bit the grass and tore their clothes. I knew that these were mourning relatives of the dead girl, and the impact of the scene on my already guilty conscience was overwhelming. I staggered away from the place and somehow found my way back to my miserable abode.

Fortunately the two men from the mission had arrived. One would be my cook, and stay at the hut; the other was to follow me, carrying my equipment when I went around. The teacher now joined me again and tried to hold me back. The houses of the village were far apart, he argued; it would be too hot and tiresome to walk in the sun on the stony paths. He should have thought of this when he allowed the children to run home! I was far too upset to heed his words and ran from one place to the other finding the little patients prostrated in the darkest corners of the huts, half crazed from fear, hunger and thirst. Nobody had dared to go near them since they returned. Many of them were hot with fever. Malaria is endemic in the African bush and tends to flare up after physical or emotional stress, so I dispensed antimalaria drugs, heart strengthening medication and my panacea, sugar-water. I was greatly relieved to see that most of the little ones responded well, and once they had lost their fear, they got up and walked around. They were soon out of danger. As the teacher translated my instructions, I could see the expressions—fear and hope, suspicion and trust—shifting on the mothers' faces. When dusk crept over the dry land I had seen more than half of all the children, and there had been no further alarming news about the others. I dragged my feet back to my quarters and forced myself to eat some of the chicken and rice the cook had prepared. Some people had brought a few eggs. That was always a sign of good will and it made me feel better.

Night in my mudhut. The bed was a wooden frame with twisted ropes strung over it, covered with thin mats. A true paradise for bugs. Of what kind it was too tiresome to find out. They were biting anyway, and sleep would not come. The moon shone down through cracks in the roof and the tropical night was full of noises. Somewhere a child was crying. Animals seemed to crawl in the grass; a hyena was howling somewhere out there, and voices reached me from a hut across the school yard. There the little girl that died the first evening had lived. I heard a few sobs, and then, when the moon was high up in the sky, the mourning chant was sung by the fire in front of the hut. A man's voice—maybe it was the father: "Ay—ay—ay—eeee...ma—va—oooo...je—le—maooo..." and then heartbreaking sobs. There was a strange beauty in the song as the voice rose and fell, reaching up in melancholy towards the moon. I lay there spellbound. Hours passed and there was no end to it. Little by little the voice seemed to penetrate my body. It opened up one door of resistance after the other, allowing heavy, guilt-ridden thoughts to crowd into my mind. What was I doing in Africa? What right did I have to be here, unwittingly bringing unhappiness and death to these people whose language and customs I did not even understand? An irresistible impulse made me sit up. I wanted to walk over to the bereaved father, say something, cry with him —but I did not dare to do so. Instead I fell back into heavy thoughts. The children must have been much more afraid than I had realized. If only I had looked after them better myself!

The teacher had probably not even understood my instructions. That night cast doubt on my whole effort in Africa. I realized how dubious was the blessing of mass treatment if poorly organized. I stopped trusting Western medicine when practiced among non-Western people where many unknown factors are at work. It was a night I would never forget. Towards morning the sing-song died away and there was even some laughter. Exhausted I fell into a deep sleep.

Another arduous day—wandering through the bush; sweating in the sun; looking up the children; examining feeble patients; listening to anxious hearts; giving out medicine and reassuring apprehensive parents. The children I had treated on the previous day were recovering well and looked forward to the cherished sugar-water. The ones I had not yet seen needed help urgently. One of the last families to visit lived far away on a hill. Tired, I climbed the steep path to find the people there hostile and upset. A little girl who had also been at the mission for treatment was dying, they claimed. Inside the hut it was dark and the air was heavy from smoke and from the many people watching the girl. In the flickering light of the fire I saw the child lying on the floor, semiconscious. Convulsive jerks shook her body. Her skin was burning hot and her lips cracked and dry. I tried to give her something to drink but she grimaced and could not swallow. I asked the women to carry her outside and to place her on a mat in the shadow. They did so very reluctantly and after much arguing among themselves.

The child moaned. She was pale, and deep furrows were drawn around her mouth and nose. Her eyes rolled upwards. This was indeed a dying child! Kneeling down beside her I prepared a syringe for an injection to strengthen her heart. Suddenly the air seemed to be tight with danger. I looked up. A group of men with spears and bush knives stood around me, their faces sinister. My companions and most of the women had disappeared. "No more injections! My daughter has had enough," said the girl's father in Swahili. His voice was threatening and the men closed in on me. "If the child dies, I will die, too," the thought flashed through my mind. "They will kill me, because they are afraid." My stomach tightened; I felt weak and nauseated. There was no escape. My thoughts were racing. The child must not die! I had the same medicine in tablet form so I forced my hands to calm down and crushed a tablet in a spoon with water. With utmost care, very slowly, I poured it between the clenched teeth of the girl, who seemed to be almost dead. I remembered her well; she had been one of the wildest children in the bunch. Sweat was pouring down my back and I avoided looking up at the men.

Next I had to bring her fever down. Medicine would not do as I did not dare to let her swallow the bitter malaria tablets lest she throw up. I asked for some cloth, but as nobody made a move, I took off my shawl, dipped it in water and wrapped it around her legs. I also cooled her front with water, and as I repeatedly urged her to swallow the cardiac medicine, it appeared to me that the little girl understood my plight. She seemed to make every effort to cooperate. After a long time—it seemed like hours—her pulse slowed down and the fever receded. There were moments when I thought I was going to faint myself, but the instinct of self-preservation kept me alert as I watched every change in the patient. Towards evening she drank some sugar-water and then opened her eyes and smiled at me. Like the sun breaking through clouds, the tension around me eased. The threatening posture of the men relaxed, somebody laughed, the women lit the fires, and everybody in the yard went about doing their daily tasks. I looked at the girl's father. He too was smiling as we both watched the now peacefully sleeping child.

The teacher came back and after having assured the father that the girl would live, I picked up my belongings and made it down the hill. Waves of weakness went through my aching body and I had to stop from time to time to regain strength. "You must be awfully tired," the teacher said shyly. My companions had to help me along the stony path in the dark and upon reaching my quarters I was too exhausted to eat. Still trembling I lay in bed anxiously listening into the night. Did I hear cries in the distance? A message that the girl had died after all? But the night was quiet. Even the people by the school did not lament. They talked together in low voices; probably they discussed the day's events. Steps outside the door. I stiffened in fear. "Listen to me," a woman's voice called. It was friendly. "Would you like one of us to stay with you? Maybe you feel afraid alone in the hut?" I declined, saying that I was not scared, but it gave me a warming feeling. They did táke me for a human being after all. I began to calm down and finally fell asleep with the vague idea that I had atoned. It had been my life for the little girl's life. She lived, so I could live—it seemed fair.

I strained my ears for mourning chants when I slowly climbed the hill the next day. Should I dare to go there? Everything remained quiet, so the girl must have lived through the night. She was sitting up when I entered the hut, eagerly awaiting my sugar-water and she drank whatever I offered her. I viewed the child with fondness and a kind of pride. That little wild kid surely wanted to live—just as much as I did!

There were no more complications with the children but I stayed on for a few days more, just to make sure, before I sent for the Father. People now came to see me for all kinds of ailments, and as much as I enjoyed their trust, it was very trying. There was no end to the work. As tired as I was, I did not dare to refuse any of the cases, lest suspicion and hostility should flare up again. They came at dawn and often did not allow me time to eat. Only nightfall ended my work since everybody understood that I needed daylight to treat the sick. Never before had I greeted evenings with such relief. When the Father arrived one afternoon he found me in the midst of a squabbling crowd. He turned pale until he realized that people were fighting among themselves to get to me for treatment. Whilst we quickly packed up, we tried to console the loudly protesting patients. We invited the people to take their sick to the mission; I would treat them there. But even when I had climbed onto the motorbike, people hung on to my clothes and begged for medicine. Again I felt the sting of bad conscience. All these people had come to me for help. Was it right to turn my back on them? This was always the dilemma facing one who dared to challenge life and death in the African bush. Wherever one arrives, some severely ill persons will survive because they get the right medicine; wherever one leaves others will die because they cannot get it. Wearily I closed my eyes as the village and its people disappeared behind me in the bush. Would I ever be able to accept the role I had to play in these people's destiny?

8
Poisoning and Witchcraft: Two Fates

It was a hot dry day, but pleasant enough for the long, bumpy drive in the landrover. I was headed for the small out-post mission of Ngoheranga on the other side of the Ulanga River—a place where I had never been before. I had been asked to look over the medical supplies there and to see how the young dresser was managing the dispensary on his own.

As usual the mission was situated on a hill, and big mango trees gave shadow to the main building. Both the little church and the mission house were built of locally-made bricks which the diligent Capuchins had manufactured themselves from the red clay of the plains. Unfinished bricks in their forms were spread out in long rows beside the half-underground kiln and huge stacks of heavy logs were piled up, ready to be used for the firing. At night the glow from the fires shone through the openings and cast shadows of the men watching. Nicely built small brick houses along the road showed that some of the Africans had caught on to the idea of building brick houses rather than the traditional mud huts. The bricks stood up much better in the onslaught of the monsoon rains.

When I arrived it was towards evening and people were

still waiting for treatment outside the dispensary. The young dresser greeted me with a shy smile but a quick glance inside the room told me that he did not fully understand what sterilization implies. He had sterilized his syringes and needles all right, but when the boiled water in the little pot cooled off, he had picked up the instruments with his fingers and placed the used needles together with the clean ones without boiling the water again. The dresser was a friendly man, however, and appeared eager to learn. While I tried to explain the essentials of sterilization in Swahili, the room darkened from the many curious people peeping in through the door and window. I waved at them to move away, as we needed the daylight, but I might just as well have tried to chase away flies. They only laughed at me as they packed the doorway and pressed as many heads as possible through the window. The air became sticky and it was unbearably hot in the little room.

Suddenly there was a commotion outside and the door and window cleared as people gathered in the yard. Somebody called for *Mama Mganga* and we went out to see what was going on. Amidst the crowd was the village chief, half carrying, half dragging a crying man. The man looked around with terror in his eyes. He vomited and screamed with pain, pulling up his knees and pressing his hands against his stomach as he yelled, "*Uchavi—uchavi*—my wife used *uchavi* against me. I am dying, I am poisoned." While I was listening to his pounding heart, the chief told us that the man had become violently sick after eating some food prepared by his wife. The man seemed in agony and sweat was pearling on his forehead; the people around waited for me to do something. Nervously I looked for a suitable medicine. The only thing I could find was some tincture of opium. Thinking that the man was dying of fear more than anything else, I poured about twenty drops into a mug of water and bade him drink it. He was shaking so violently that we had to support his head and hold the cup to his lips. The effect of the opium was dramatic. His stomach pain vanished as if brushed away by a hand-stroke. The man looked at me in amazement, his body relaxed and his head sank to the ground. "The pain is gone," he sighed with relief. After a while he dozed off and his friends lifted him up and carried him home.

After dinner when I mentioned the incident to the Father, he told me that the local people were extremely afraid of *uchavi,* witchcraft. They attribute any death, from illness or by accident, to witchcraft, black magic, bad spirits or poisoning. When a person becomes seriously ill, everybody must pay him a visit. The one who fails to do so will inevitably be suspected of having caused the illness by witchcraft or in some other way. Sometimes a witch hunt would start. The medicine man would prepare a potion for every adult person in the village to drink in public. The one who refused to drink or who vomited from it would be singled out as a wizard, and such a person might be chased away from the village. When the Father first came, he had felt somewhat threatened until he was assured that *uchavi* and poison never work against whites.

Later that evening the chief returned and asked the dresser and me to see the same man who was again in great pain. When we came to his hut, many people were assembled there expecting him to die. We could hear the unhappy man's cries long before we entered his home. He was crouching on his bed, holding on to a friend and waving his hand in front of his eyes whimpering: "I cannot see, I am blind, please give me that medicine or I'll die!" A few drops of opium produced the anticipated relief and when the man had calmed down, the chief asked him to tell what happened. Uneasy, the man muttered that he could only tell it to the chief alone. His wife, other relatives, the dresser and I, all made moves to leave. But the chief with an authoritarian gesture motioned us to stay and we sat down quietly. After a little while the man lifted his head and asked, "Are we alone now?" "Yes, you can talk now," the chief answered. The sick man seemed indeed unable to see. Or was it a kind of game they played? The man leaned towards the chief and spoke in a low voice, but loud enough for everybody to hear. He confessed that he had been unfaithful to his wife. She had found out and become very angry, threatening him with *uchavi* if he did not stop seeing the other woman. But he had not heeded her warning. Today when he came back from the other woman, his wife had cooked a porridge and invited him to eat with her. He hesitated. "Why is the porridge so bitter?" he wanted to know after having tasted it. "Just eat, the porridge is as sweet as can be," his wife retorted. When he still hesitated the woman laughed at him, calling him a coward. He saw no way of getting out of it and reluctantly ate the porridge. Immediately afterwards he felt knifing pains in his stomach. Convinced that he had been poisoned, he rushed out and screamed for help. That was when the chief brought him to the dispensary.

I was deeply interested in what was going on. I felt I was witness to a kind of village court. Everybody was listening with grave and intense faces. I looked at the wife. She sat motionless at the bedside, a strange smile on her face. Her mother who sat beside her was wringing her hands in despair. Both women knew very well that if the man died his young wife would be branded as a witch and chased out of the village or even killed. Due to the chief's wise precaution many witnesses had heard the husband's accusations and it would be difficult for her and her family to defend her. But she showed no sign of fear. Maybe she had not done anything wrong after all? If she had only wished to scare her husband, I thought, she had certainly succeeded.

Fortunately the man did not die. The next day his eyesight was restored and he felt no more pain. What final arrangement he made with his wife, I do not know, but he sent me a big, fat hen for having saved his life. A few days later he came to thank me personally. He pulled me aside and asked secretively if he could possibly have some more of that wonderful medicine to take home. The rascal! I think he just wanted to have the remedy at hand should he want to cheat on his wife again!

* * * * * *

Quick steps in the dark—how I dreaded them for I knew

75

that somebody was in distress! We were sitting outside after a day's hard work. I liked this habit of the Capuchins, to rest in garden chairs after dinner, cooling off in the evening breeze, looking at the stars and leisurely talking about whatever came to mind. But then there were these steps. *"Hodi,"* someone announced his presence, waiting for an invitation to come closer. *"Karibu, shida gani*—Come here and tell us your trouble." The messenger came from one of the Father's workers who had taken ill. He was in great pain; could *Mama Mganga* come to see him? With a sigh I gathered up my tired limbs and went over to the dispensary for my instruments and medicines. Then I followed the Father and the messenger along the narrow path leading down the hill. We were waving our kerosene lamps and whistling to scare away any *kibokos,* hippopotamuses, which might be around. One could always hear them grunt down at the river where they were grazing at night. Light would sometimes arouse their curiosity and these huge animals were rather dangerous. Easily frightened, they would run down to the river to hide in the water, crushing anybody in their way. I had seen a patient in the hospital who had been terribly mauled by a hippo, and I shuddered there in the dark, anxiously listening for the snores of those wild beasts.

Fortunately the man did not live far away. I knew who he was; a friendly person, always smiling. Obviously very fond of the Father, he made himself useful around the mission. He was a strong, middle-aged man, who had built himself a nice house of bricks with several windows. The wide yard was always swept clean and his wife had even planted some flowers around their compound. They were both glad when we entered. The man was indeed very sick and he lay prostrate on his bed, his head thrust backwards. He moaned with pain as he stretched out his hand to thank us for coming. His hand was hot and dry. The timid young wife with a sleepy little child on her hip told us that he had fallen ill by the river where he had been for a few days to buy fish. The market was a few hours march through the bush, and when returning home this morning he had complained about aches and pains all over his body. The whole day he had refused to eat. Now he suffered from unbearable headaches and had therefore sent for us. I was alarmed. This looked like beginning meningo-encephalitis. I had seen sporadic outbreaks of this contagious disease in other places and knew there was no reliable cure. The rate of recovery was not very high, but I hoped that this man had a better chance as he was unusually healthy and strong.

In the following days I went to his house twice a day to treat him with the available medicine. On one day he seemed to improve, but on the next his condition worsened again. With great sorrow we saw our friend wasting away. Relatives and friends began to arrive to show their concern. They sat in the yard waiting to see which turn the illness would take. Herpes blisters appeared around the sick man's mouth and nose, a sure sign of viral infection. Continuous pain in his back and head exhausted the poor man, and his hearing began to fail. But he preserved his dignity and I admired his endurance and courage. In the evenings he became delirious, a fact which highly alarmed people outside. It became an ordeal for me to cross the yard. The people would fall silent and I could feel their disappointment and anxiety as they followed me with their eyes. They gradually realized that I did not have control over the illness.

One day I noticed that the window-holes were plugged with old rags. Since the sick man in his feverish condition needed fresh air, I asked his wife to free the windows again. But she refused with visible embarrassment. On our way home the dresser explained that the people thought the sick man was possessed by evil spirits, probably sent by ancestors in retaliation for having built for himself such an untraditionally big house. African huts are small and have no windows because spirits try to sneak in through every hole in the walls. The huts have only one opening, since spirits never use the same entrance as living beings. By plugging the windows of the sick man's house, people hoped to keep the evil spirits outside. I felt quite upset about what I heard, suspecting that envy of his big house might also account for what they said and did. Once, as I bent over the sick man, he grabbed my arm and urgently whispered, "Please protect me from these people, don't let them carry me away." I looked at his wife for an explanation, but she sat in stubborn silence as usual, tending her child as if she had not heard a word.

The small amount of medicines at the little dispensary was running low. I would have to get new supplies from the Danish mission hospital far away on the other side of the river. I decided to go myself in order to consult the physician there regarding my patient. The evening before I left a small group of old men came to see me. They stood in a row before me, politely asking my permission to move the sick man out of his house. I remembered his pleading and firmly said "No." He who cried out in pain upon the slightest touch could not possibly tolerate being carried away from his bed. Haltingly the old men expressed their fear that the patient would not recover in that "big" house. Finally when they realized that I was not going to give in, the little delegation of worried men left with a sad expression on their faces.

Driven by my intense wish to help this friendly patient who trusted me, I traveled as fast as I could. Nevertheless it took me several days before I could return with the medicine. The physician in the hospital had essentially confirmed my treatment. I did not even bother to eat or rest before I hurried down the hill to the sick man's house with new supplies and new hopes. The yard was silent, the house empty. Nobody greeted me at the door. I looked forlornly around. Where was my patient? I must have looked pretty sad, because neighbors hiding in their huts finally sent a woman out to talk to me. We sat down under a tree and she slowly explained to me what had happened. The old men had used my absence to convince the patient's relatives that the only way he could recover was to take him back to the place where he had contracted the illness. Apparently he had quarrelled with the fishermen about the price of the fish down there by the river. Maybe they had used *uchavi* against him, or maybe bush-spirits had come to possess him on the way home. Only the local medicine man could find out and cure the patient. The relatives had made a stretcher and carried him away the night after I left.

Downcast, I walked up the hill. There was not much hope for him any more and I felt as if I had failed him somehow. It did not take long before it was known in the village that *Mama Mganga* was back again. Only a few hours later the same little troop of old men marched up to the mission and once more asked to see me. The sick man had not recovered and now they feared he would die without my help. At first I refused. I was angry and they well knew why. After the long journey to fetch medicine, I did not feel prepared to walk for hours through the night to where they had moved the patient against my advice. But the old men looked so dismal I could not turn them down. With tears in their eyes they said they had only done what they thought was right and what tradition taught them to do.

While the Father and I were stumbling along in the dark, I thought how painful it must have been for the sick man to be carried on this stony path. But that was not all. I thought of the ordeal that must have followed when he was brought to the medicine man for treatment. Although I had not met this particular medicine man, I had an idea of how indigenous healers worked. I could visualize how, without giving the sick man time to rest, the family would have built a huge fire and sent for the medicine man. They would have wrapped the patient up tightly in a blanket and placed him, like a parcel, close to the fire. There he would lie on the ground, uncomfortably, sweating and listening for hours to drumming, singing and dancing while the medicine man worked himself up into a trance. Exhausted as he was, the sick man would not have been allowed to sleep. Once the medicine man thought he had found out the sick-making agency, the actual treatment procedure would start, adding new suffering to the sick man's pain. In spite of his head and back aching, they would have sat him up and carried him around the fire. The medicine man would ask him many questions and massage and manipulate his stiff body. Since the illness manifested itself mainly in the head, the medicine man, assuming that the sick-making spirits could be reached through the natural openings, might have blown smoke from burning herbs into his nostrils, or dripped a potion into his ears. I had a certain respect for indigenous healers and their art, but in a case of meningitis, I could only foresee more suffering from this kind of treatment.

My thoughts were interrupted as we finally reached the little fishing village by the river where they had carried the sick man. There we found our friend. What a miserable sight! The once so dignified and clean man was lying on the wet mud floor of a little hut, wrapped in dirty rags. Whimpering faintly, he did not seem to recognize what was going on around him. He did wake up for a moment as I gave him an injection and he eagerly drank the water I poured between his swollen lips. As is often the case when a person has fever and for a reason I never could understand, the people had withheld water from him, and his body was severely dehydrated. There was not much I could do. His pulse was faint and he was obviously nearing his end. I stepped aside when I had finished with him and let the priest do his job. The women's wailing mingled with the sad prayers of the men. The light from the small oil lamps was flickering on distressed faces as the priest prepared for the extreme unction. When we left, our friend, relieved by my medicine and consoled by the priest, had fallen into a peaceful slumber. But already before we reached the Mission, a messenger caught up with us. The sick man had passed away.

Lonely *kilio* from a woman through the nights down there by the brick house. Was there anything more I could have done?

9
The Epidemic

Like so many natural phenomena, the rainy season in tropical Africa is dramatic and full of exciting events. Towards the end of the dry season after unusually hot days when a merciless sun forces people to linger in the shadows, clouds begin to gather and before nightfall there is a cataclysm of lightning, rain and thunder. After having endured the dusty dry weather with its scorching heat, everybody enjoys the cool rainwater running down face and body. The people smile and laugh as they watch the little children running naked out of the huts to splash and dance in the streaming rain.

Traveling then became a special adventure, but I liked the challenge of coping with all the unpredictable obstacles on the way: dashing through shallow streams that flooded the road and hoping our landrover would make it through, enduring the laughter of the onlookers when it got stuck, watching eager helpers pulling the vehicle out and waiting in the sun until the motor was dry again. At other times, we would glide quietly among the trees over the flooded fields in a dug-out canoe, observing the teeming life in the water, half afraid a turbulent current, a tree trunk, or the back of a hippopotamus

81

might overturn the fragile craft.

From Ifakara the road to the distant mission outpost of Taweta had to cross the many tributaries of the Ulanga River. Mission stations were close enough so that one could travel from one to the other within a day, even during the rainy season.

One evening after a rainy day on that road I arrived at Iragua where one Father managed a small station alone. In his solitude he was always happy to receive guests and felt especially relieved when the visitor was a nurse or a doctor. He was eager to show me some of the seriously ill patients whom he had tried to help as best he could. I had hardly time to get out of the car before he took me to his little dispensary to see two small children. Their mothers had brought them to the mission after an exhausting march through the bush. They told the Father that some evil spirit had befallen their village and caused illness among the children. The people were in great fear because their medicine man had been unable to find the cause of this calamity and was unable to treat the afflicted children. Most parents did not dare to take their sick children on the long arduous journey through the bush, but these two mothers had braved the rain and brought their sick babies to the mission for help. As soon as I saw the skin rash of the children and their sore eyes and heard their rattling cough I knew that they had measles. For the malaria-infested and poorly nourished youngsters in the African bush an epidemic of measles was disastrous. The physically weak children quickly succumbed to pneumonia, a frequent complication of the disease. One single shot of penicillin, however, would often suffice to clear up the lungs and save the child's life. This was the case with the two little ones I thus treated at the mission, and the mother showed profound gratitude when I visited the children again the following morning. We discussed what to do about the epidemic and estimated that there were about fifty families with small children in the village the women had come from. We decided to take a trip to the village and to see what we could do. Since it was the rainy season and the bush was full of mosquitoes, tse-tse flies and all sorts of snakes and other dangerous creatures, we did not dare to stay out overnight. If we took the motor bike and started out before dawn, we would have time to spend a few hours in the village and still return to the mission before dark. I got the instruments ready, gathered up all the penicillin I could find in the little dispensary, and with that we set out early next morning.

There is something unforgettably beautiful about the early morning hours in tropical Africa. The threatening darkness of the night gradually recedes as a pale stripe of light appears on the horizon. An intense silence accompanies the dawn; the air is still and crisp with no wind rustling through the trees and the grass is cool and wet. Gradually the sky takes on an intense red and yellow coloring and suddenly there is the sun in all its glory, spreading warmth and light over the land, caressing the chilled skin with its warming rays. The new day is born as the jubilant birds break the silence with their songs, announcing their mere joy of being alive, knowing nothing of the sorrow and suffering the day might bring.

We too were filled with happiness at taking part in the great overture of the awakening day as we drove along the narrow path up and down the hills through the forest. We felt good there in the morning sun, knowing that we were on a mission to help suffering children. The small motor bike was not heavy and could easily be carried when shallow floods from the last night's rain blocked our way. Where the swollen rivers had washed away fragile bridges, friendly Africans ferried us across in their canoes. They laughed merrily while balancing the motor bike in the tiny dug-outs and were amused about my fear lest the medical supplies should get wet.

We reached the village towards noon and were greeted by the high-pitched trills the women sound when announcing a happy event. As usual, everybody received us with absorbing curiosity. The women laughed at their children screaming with fear at seeing the white strangers. They soon made room for the elders who greeted us ceremoniously while their wives arranged for us a meal of rice and chicken under a big tree. While we were eating the chief spoke about the mysterious disease. He told us that some children had already died and he thanked the Father for bringing *Mama Mganga* to treat the afflicted children. Ill at ease, I noticed a growing crowd of women with sad-looking youngsters hanging in slings on their backs. Seeing how the flock increased by the minute, I knew there would be more than enough work to do, and while the Father was still talking with the men, I spread out my instruments on a clean sheet I had brought along. I asked some of the women to make a small fire and to keep the water boiling which was needed continuously to sterilize the few injection needles I had. Since there were no tables or chairs in the whole village, treatment had to be given right there on the ground so the women knelt down around me. Each was eager to have her child treated first and they all got in my way as I tried to hold the terrified children. I called the Father to help me; but he was not at all fit for the role of a nurse. He held the children most awkwardly, turning his face away with a pitiful grimace when the injection was given. A few times the needle nearly broke in a child's behind because the Father jerked and dropped the child when it let out a howl. The poor Father was more a hindrance than a help and I became impatient with him, which of course made matters worse.

I noted the miserable condition of the children. Most of them showed shallow respiration with flapping nostrils and many coughed up bloody froth, a sign of acute pneumonia. It was not even necessary to use the stethoscope; my hand placed flat on the child's burning chest could feel the roughness of breathing inside. Although one shot of penicillin could work wonders, I realized that some of the little ones were already beyond remedy. More and more people arrived and for each child treated there seemed to be two more coming. Finally I had to face the fact that there was not enough penicillin for all of them. I felt hot and cold; we were surrounded by moaning, crying and coughing children. What a miserable situation! I was inclined to withhold treatment from the dying ones and to

84

give the precious medication to those who had a better chance to survive. But how could I explain that to their mothers? Impossible!

I began to mix distilled water with the penicillin and to give sufficient doses to only some of the children. I felt like a criminal, and my tension mounted as the penicillin supply diminished. The mothers sensed my uneasiness and anxiously pushed forward. At last the Father stood up and declared we had to leave. A storm of protest arose. Why should some of the children get help and others not? Could we not see that the little ones would die if they did not receive the injection? The women closed the circle around us, sobbed and begged, clutching their crying, coughing children, holding them up to our faces. I looked around in amazement. Where had all the people come from? The mothers must have run for miles through the bush with their sick children. There was no way that I could treat them all. Clouds were gathering in the sky and the rumbling of thunder came closer. We would *have* to leave. But they did not let us. The mothers threw themselves down in front of us: "*Mama Mganga,* you cannot leave us now, please don't let my child die, help my child, it is such a good baby, can't you see how sweet it is? Why did my neighbor's child get help and you refuse my baby? What have I done wrong? Why don't you like my baby? Please give an injection to my child, just a little one and it will not die!" They grabbed our arms, blocked our way, seized the motor bike. The children howled and coughed, cried and moaned. Big drops of rain started to fall and soon we were soaking wet. The whole scene had turned into an ugly nightmare.

I had no more penicillin, but I had to do something to appease the desperate crowd. Knowing that to the mothers it was the syringe and not its contents which had the magic to save their children, I filled the empty penicillin bottles with sterile water. But the rain had extinguished the fire and the boiled water was mixed with water from above. Is rainwater clean? I wondered as I injected the thin penicillin water into the little behinds of the shivering children. The cool rain splashed the febrile naked bodies of the sick children making the skin damp like that of horses after a race. I worked in a fury as one child after the other was held before me. The mothers thanked me and their smiles burned my heart. The emotional strain, embarrassment and fatigue blurred my senses and made me confused. I vaguely remember how the lightning dazzled me and reflected on the wet bodies and that needles and bottles were washed away in the downpour. But we had to carry on to the bitter end until the last child had received its shot. Then we picked up our instruments and ran away, leaving behind a few latecomers and other sick people who had hoped to get some help.

We stumbled along in the rain full of pity for the many children we knew we had not helped, burning with shame about what we had done. With shaky hands we started the bike far away from the village. What a miserable failure, what a mockery of medicine! Tears mingled with raindrops on my face as we drove off amidst thunder and lightning. It served us right that we skidded off the road and fell into the mud. It did not matter that we lost all our equipment in the raging streams. It was good that darkness hid our faces from which the rain could not wash away the shame. I do not remember when we finally reached the mission. I only know that it was pitch dark, that we had fought our way mostly on foot and that the motor bike had been something cold to hold on to in the turbulence of rain and water and mud.

10
Mothers

Sometimes I could not stand them anymore, the mothers with their sick babies hanging there on their backs in a sling around their shoulders. Wherever I went, they were always there, waiting patiently but persistently for my attention. I could feel their presence when I talked to somebody else; I knew they were there in the mornings waiting for me to open the dispensary. I saw them running along the road, crossing the yard to intercept me when I was on my way back and forth from work. I could hear them chatting in the shadow of the trees waiting for me to come out. At any given moment a mother might step in front of me. With a movement of her shoulder she would swing the child to the front and open up the cloth that covered it and protected it from the blazing sun. A smell of sickness would fill my nose and the child, suddenly exposed to the light and to the strange sight of a white woman, would let out a wail. *"Mama Mganga, mtoto ana homa"*—the child has fever—how often did these words hit my ear!

I could not avoid the mothers; they were always asking for help, never questioning my availability, never thinking that it could be too much for me. Of course, each mother knew only her own worries; I had to know them all. With bitterness I thought that only if I dropped dead would they leave me alone. How tired I felt of washing out infected eyes and cleaning up little faces. The children seemed always to have a cold. The mucus from their noses would smear all over their face and inflame their eyes, making the eyelids swollen and painful. I used to dip a piece of cotton in the water with which I had rinsed the penicillin bottles and wipe the pus from under their eyelids. Painful as it was, one such treatment often sufficed to clear the infection. If only the mothers had cleaned the noses of their children, most of the eye infections could have been avoided. The people even grew cotton in their fields. I remember once after having gone through the smelly procedure with lots of sweaty crying children, I finally shouted in exasperation at the mothers, "Why can't you clean up the faces of the children yourselves?" They looked at me startled. A long silence followed. "But *Mama Mganga,*" said a gentle voice, "nobody ever told us to do so."

One day at noon when I was just closing the dispensary at Igota one of the mothers came running with her sick child bundled up on her back. "No, not another one," I thought and avoided looking at her. She tried to stop me on my way to lunch. She was panting and pleaded with me to see her child at once. But I was too tired. I had to draw the line somewhere. If I stopped now, other mothers would come and I would soon be too tired to eat. Everybody in the tropics is entitled to a little rest during the hottest hours of the day. If I continued to work now, my strength would be gone. How should I then face the long work hours of the afternoon? So I told her she had to wait. She sank down beside the door with her child.

When I returned to the dispensary in the afternoon, the mother was still sitting there by the door in frozen resignation, holding a lifeless child on her lap. I refused to see that the child was dead. I seized it, carried it into the treatment room, cooled the overheated body, shot a needle into the limp arm and listened to the silent chest. Life was irretrievably gone. Death had not waited for me to eat and rest.

I was still working on the corpse when the child's father entered. He gave me a quick, hostile glance before he lowered his eyes and picked up his son. He did not say a word to me but turned around and left the room, his dead child in his arms. I followed him outside. His wife sat there immobile as if made of stone. He spoke to her in a soft voice. Suddenly she leaped up with a howl and buried her teeth in his shoulder. I could see the blood trickling down his arm. He freed himself and gently sat her down. I could not bear the sight any longer and left them with their sorrow. But my hands were shaking as I continued my work. I thought I could feel the mothers' disapproval and see reproach in their soft eyes as they stood there waiting for their turn. The woman's sobs could be heard through the door and the sad scene burned on my mind. I worked frantically to wipe out my feelings of guilt. Finally the mission's landrover drove up in front of the dispensary and the Father announced that the car was ready to take me to my next assignment.

When I was sitting in the car ready to leave, another mother approached me, this time with a smiling baby on her back. She too smiled and stretched out her hand, maybe to thank me? "*Savadi Mama*—give me a present." Something exploded in my head. "Go away!" I shouted at the top of my voice. All the tension and the agony of the day was in that outburst. The woman backed off and the Father quickly started the car and drove away. I was shaking all over. The Father glanced at me from the corner of his eye. He waited until I had calmed down a bit. Then he began to talk. He told me about a friend of his who had come to Africa to work with him. He was a strong and healthy man. Eagerly he had taken on more and more tasks, not heeding the Father's warnings. Convinced that he could not become ill he carelessly accepted the invitation to stay overnight with the Africans, to eat their food and drink their water. Of course he contracted malaria, typhoid fever and who knows what else. Before the year was over he was a dead man. The Father paused for a moment and then continued, "In the African bush we have to learn to know our limits. We must be humble and not think we are like God, able to do anything we want. We must show self-discipline. Enough sleep, enough rest, enough food, caution about where we go and what we do, all this is part of keeping ourselves fit and capable. Only in this way can we be efficient and give our best to those we want to help.''

I understood the message and after a while my troubled mind and body relaxed as I looked out over the beautiful landscape. As we drove along in silence ideas slowly formed in my mind. Children here, I thought, are not necessarily born to grow up and become adults. Maybe children are born just for the sake of being children, to fill our lives with their laughter and their cries, to be cherished and embraced with love, to gladden our hearts and soften our minds. The sweetest little ones with laughing mouths and sparkling eyes may wither away in times of sickness or famine. Other children will take their place; they come and go like the seasons of the year. Just as the dry earth will give new life to plants and animals when rain is falling, so mothers will give birth to new children, generously and patiently, twelve or more during their reproductive years. But only three or four may grow up. To a mother the baby is only a possibility, not a full human being.

I had heard how mothers jokingly called their little babies *nyama*. *Nyama* is the term for animal, meat, body or matter. The phrase warns the mother not to attach herself too much to the baby. I remembered also that babies born with teeth already in their mouth, or twins, are killed right away because they are "too much like animals." They are strangled to prevent the dangerous animal spirit from leaving the baby's body and harming the mother or other family members. Thinking of it, I could now understand why a mother, having cared for her sick baby, faithfully following all my instructions, would sometimes turn suddenly away from her child and lose all interest in it. Long before I recognized it, she knew the baby was going to die.

The healthier a child is and the older it gets, the more interest a mother takes in its care. When the child starts to talk it

90

demonstrates that it is a full human being. Only when a child is four or five years old and healthy, so that it has a good chance to survive, will the mother permit herself to love it unreservedly. The mourning period for a baby is only three days; a mother might sing her *kilio*—"song of sorrow"—for about one week if the child was already walking and for up to one year if the child was grown up, the same length as for her husband or other close relatives. The length of the *kilio* time is a matter of self-discipline, and a mother has to restrain her grief for the sake of her other children. To mourn longer than the prescribed time is considered bad taste and neighbors and friends will not support it. The child I had seen that day was at least two years old—a strong looking child. If only I had . . .

Towards the evening we had to cross the Kilombero River. On the ferry an old woman caught my attention. She was sitting on deck covering her face with a black scarf. She was rocking slowly and singing faintly with quivering voice a *kilio*. From time to time she wiped her face with a corner of the cloth, sweat pearls and tears rolling down her wrinkled cheeks. People treated her with respect. They whispered that up the river a young man had been mauled by a crocodile. The old woman was his mother. Everybody went with her to a place on the other side of the river further up from where we landed where the young man's friends had bedded him in the grass. The handsome youth was lying motionless. His eyes were closed and from several large wounds blood trickled to the ground. When the old mother saw her son lying there lifeless she tore her clothes apart and threw herself backwards, hitting the ground with an awful thud. She pulled out bunches of grass, filled her hands with sand and poured it over her head. She sprang up and would have thrown herself down again had friends not caught her and held her firmly.

We stood there spellbound in the setting sun. We had just witnessed a strange and beautiful scene; an archaic expression of human emotion, an ancient gesture of grief and sorrow.

11
The Mwali Girls

One day in Igota as I was dozing on my bed in the midday heat, I heard faint knocking at my door. I tried to ignore it, but as the knocking persisted, I had to get up and open the door. This time it was a boy—a school boy as I saw from his uniform. Noticing my annoyance he nearly lost his courage. He stuttered something about his brother being ill. "I can't bear to see him like this any longer." The little guy burst into tears. I tried to distract him on our way to the village, but the tears continued to flow down his cheeks.

Many people had gathered in the yard of his home so I knew the situation was serious. I had to bend down to get through the narrow entrance and found myself in a dark room with a small fire burning on the floor. There was a peculiar smell in the hut. When my eyes got used to the dark I saw with horror something like a living skeleton on a straw mat. The skin of someone who must have been a young man was hanging loosely over the bones. Only the lower legs and feet were swollen to double their size. At the foot of the mat the boy's mother sat rocking and humming her mourning song, the white mourning paint already on her face. There was an unfriendly attitude in the room. "Why did you not send for me before?" I asked into the silence. Nobody answered, but the suffering boy looked at me with pain in his dull eyes. I gave him some water and as he gulped it down I could not help asking, "Did you not want my help?" But I regretted my question right away. An ironical glimmer in the boy's eyes showed that he had heard me, and the hostile silence in the room persisted. What on earth could I do? A little cross was hanging on a chain around his bony neck. Would he want me to call a priest, I suggested, trying nervously to break the silence. A sound like the rattling of dry leaves in the wind came from the boy's lips. His father bent over him and then gave a sullen nod, but not a word was said. I felt so unwanted that I turned around and left the hut. The schoolboy was waiting outside and on the way back I showered him with questions. I was angry too. How was it possible that a young man had been left lying sick for a long time so close to the mission and I had not been called to help as long as there had still been a chance? The schoolboy hung his head and instead of answering all my questions he simply told his brother's story.

The young man had been working away from home in another village. There he had tried to seduce a *mwali.* I knew that *mwali* was what the people of the Ulanga district called the young girls for a period of time after their menstrual cycle had started. In this period of transition from child to woman a girl is believed to have special powers and is considered dangerous to anybody but a few close relatives. To protect herself as well as others from the risks of contact, she is secluded in a hut, attended to only by old women. The schoolboy told me that his brother had been observed by the girl's father as he sneaked into her seclusion hut. When the boy ran away, he heard the angry father shout a threat at him, "Just wait, the *mwali* will send you an evil spirit which will suck out your blood." The boy was scared stiff and when he shortly afterwards contracted diarrhea he was convinced that the *mwali* was causing it with her supernatural power. He gave up his job and hurried home in panic. His family was no less frightened when they heard what had happened. Convinced that a sucking spirit was slowly killing their son, the grief-stricken parents did not even bother sending for my help. The medicine man was consulted but could not help the boy against such a curse, and everybody then accepted the illness as fate. Finally the young brother, who had been exposed to Western schooling, mustered enough courage to approach me and ask me to help. Now I understood why my young escort was crying so bitterly and I promised to do what I could. But the young man died shortly afterwards without the parents allowing me to see him again.

Time passed but I could not forget the tragic fate of that young boy, who had to die because everybody expected him to; a phenomenon which has been called *voodoo* death. I became very curious to find out more about the *mwali* and the power they seemed to have over people's minds and lives. Since I was a woman, there were fewer difficulties in accepting my help than that of a male physician and consequently I was often asked to see a *mwali* in her seclusion hut. Eager as I was to learn as much as possible about these young girls, I always tried to avail myself of these opportunities, even when it meant marching long distances through the bush. Through these visits to sick *mwalis* and by questioning women patients who had themselves been *mwali,* I came to know more about them and their ordeals than other outsiders.

When a young girl finds herself with her first menstrual bleeding, custom is that she goes to a lonely place in the bush not far from her village. There she is to squat on the ground and cry loudly until she is ceremoniously found and led back to the village. The crying marks the end of childhood and the beginning of the *mwali* period. And indeed she has reason to cry. Gone are the happy days of playing with other children, the evenings eating and joking with the family and listening to stories around the fire, gone the closeness with her mother whom she used to follow around and help with the daily tasks of cooking and looking after small children. Until now she had been everybody's favorite, receiving love and affection from the whole family.

Little girls are doted upon, since having daughters means wealth to the family. Men have to pay a high bridal price which benefits the bride's whole family. Therefore the little girls are looked after well; they are the family's investment if they grow up and reach the marriageable age of a *mwali.* During childhood they have much freedom. They wander at will to the huts of relatives and look upon all sisters of their mother as additional mothers. "Little mother" is what they call mother's younger sisters and "big mother" her older sisters. All the children of these mothers look upon each other as brothers and sisters, play together and receive equal care in all the homes. Mother's brothers' children are not as close and the same is true of father's sisters' children, since these cousins may marry each other. The mother's oldest brother holds most authority over the children; he has to sanction marriages and receives the biggest share of the bridal price. He watches ardently over the *mwali* that she is kept secluded, properly instructed and protected, so that she will become a well-bred bride, wife, and mother, and therefore secure a high bridal price.

The girl sitting in the bush cries out of apprehension and fear. Before her lies a long and strenuous time. She will be lonely and scared in the darkened hut where she will sit passively long boring hours without being allowed to stand up erect or speak out loud. Her only company will be her grandmother and old aunts from her family. They will teach her what she needs to know about married life, how to please her husband, how to become and stay pregnant, give birth and care for her baby. They will pinch her when she appears inattentive and beat her for disobedience or laziness. In a crouched posture she will have to weave mats and do other manual work. Since dark skin is looked upon as "dirty" by the old people, the attendants will wash and scrub the *mwali* daily, hoping that her skin will become lighter. Because of the supernatural powers a *mwali* possesses, she is not allowed to see the sun. Her power is not only a threat to other people from whom she must be isolated, but may also be fatal to herself if she does not carefully follow the advice of her guardians or if she unwittingly breaks one of the many taboos which rule her life. For years she may not be allowed to venture outside her hut in daylight, only stepping out during the dark hours of the night, never facing anyone but the old women. She may never speak loudly, only whisper necessary words into the guardian's ear; never walk upright, only crawl inside the hut, or move with deeply bent head when taking her little stroll at night. The more lively and independent a girl she was, the harder the old women will work on her "to break her spirit," which is deemed necessary for making her a good wife and mother. The intention, I was told, is to create a subdued, obedient and subservient woman, whatever hardship may be necessary to reach that goal. Therefore she cries anxiously there in the bush as the custom demands.

The first person who hears the crying and recognizes the girl will hasten to her mother and call out: "Your daughter has become a *mwali.*" Mother will drop whatever she is doing and with rising excitement run from one neighbor to the next, proudly announcing the glad tiding, "My daughter is a *mwali.*" Soon her women friends will accompany her to the place where the young girl is sitting and with shouts of joy they will return to the village with mother and daughter. Immediately the men in the family will be called home to build the hut that is going to be the girl's prison. They encircle it with a high fence and prepare for the feast which will mark her state as a *mwali.* During the feast she is carried in procession on the shoulder of a man around the huts of the village, followed by weeping and laughing women and finally escorted into her new compound. There darkness and fear, loneliness and boredom, scary rituals, silence and suffering will engulf her for a long, long time. The "breaking of the spirit" may take years, and sometimes young women cannot walk upright or talk long after they have been released from confinement.

The men's role in relation to the *mwali* is quite ambiguous. Male family members, including father and older

96

Mama Doctor

Mama Doctor on safari in dug-out canoe.

Ifakara Catholic Church as seen from author's window.

Hospital ward in Ifakara mission hospital.

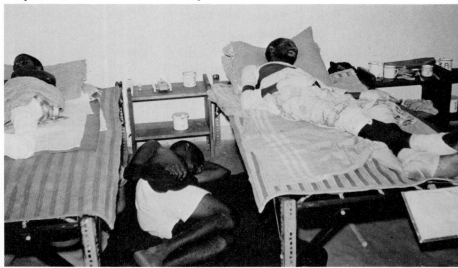

Masai father and son in the hospital.

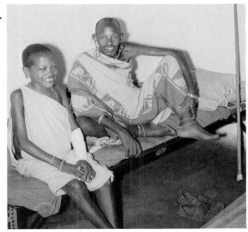

The boys at work in the laboratory.

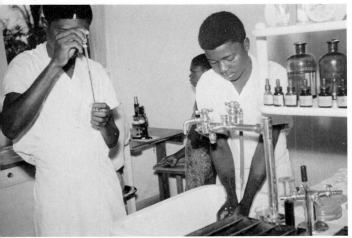

The old sister attending the outpatient clinic.

Masai runner.

Wanderers on the road. Iringa Mountains in the background.

'apogoro children and mother waiting for Mama
octor's checkup.

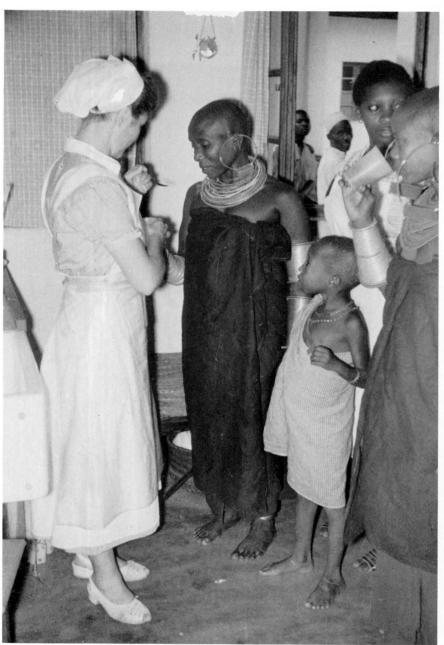

Hospital nurse with Masai women.

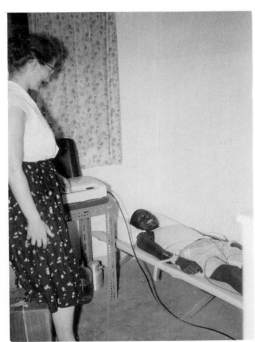

Research project underway.

asai warrior posing as driver.

Masai woman with abundant ornaments—a sign of wealth.

safari.

Mama Mganga with a friend.

Improvised clinic in the bush.

ys in Igota with their car models.

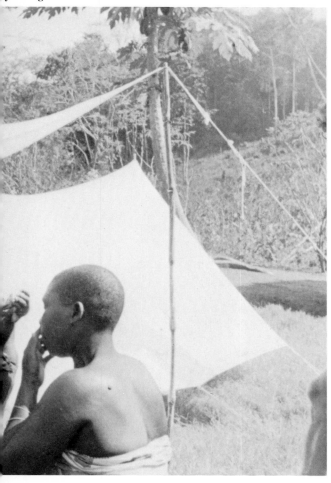

Mama Mganga, the traveling doctor.

Patients waiting outside the dispensary in Igota.

Children in the bush.

use call.

Looking for game on a hunting trip.

The ferry over Kilombero.

Bush doctor arrives!

**Sick and hungry children
cared for by nuns.**

Safari. Mama Mganga wading through water during rainy season.

Car trouble on a safari.

Leprosy wound. From the mission's leprosy village.

Young friends.

Sister serving milk.

Ifakara nurse in the village.

Mother with child.

Mama Mganga with
girlfriend.

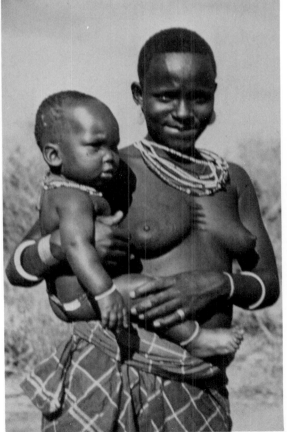

Waterhole in the bush.

Foothill of the Mahenge Mountains.

...e rainy season is coming.

...asai waiting at the ferry by Kilombero River.

Apprehensive villagers coming to
Luhombero mission.

Native healer and his wife.

My medicine man friend.

Wolfgang Jilek.

Wangindo hunters with poisonous arrows.

Wolfgang Jilek.

The slain lion with the ancestral spirit.

Kwiro Mission in Mahenge.

Sunday after Mass.

Wedding at the Mission.

...ma Doctor with dwarf antelope, the *dik-dik*.

Mother with two sick children.

The invincible diviner at his *ludewa*.

Everyday work in the secluded schoolyard.

A "housemother" with her schoolchildren.

Calamity on the road.

Sewing class at the mission.

Father with his epileptic son who was wounded in the fire.

old nurse with
kifafa patients.

Mama Mganga with some of her *kifafa* patients.

Wapogoro mother with child.

brothers must avoid any contact with her, lest their crops should fail and their game hunts be spoiled. But young men outside the family often make it a sport to try to seduce the *mwali*. A boy has to be extremely cautious, cunning and courageous to take such risks. It often needs weeks of secret observation before he finds out the times when the guardians leave the girl. He must then sneak in unseen and win the *mwali* over. If he succeeds in making the girl pregnant, then the girl's family is very much ashamed and the attendants become the laughing stock of the whole village. Then the best solution for everybody is for the boy to marry the girl—a way of securing a cheap bride since the parents cannot ask the full bridal price for a "spoiled" *mwali*. Actually the whole affair does not harm the girl herself. She is assured of another suitor, even if the child's father should not want to marry her, since she has shown her ability to become pregnant. No blame is put on her and pregnancy will certainly end her confinement as she is now an expecting mother and not a *mwali* any more. The boy, however, risks a severe beating by the guardians. The infuriated old ladies will spare no torture, and he is lucky if he gets away with a beating and the ridicule of his friends.

Sometimes when a young man has been accepted as husband-to-be of the *mwali* but is unable to come up with the full bridal price as yet, he is allowed to visit the girl in her confinement hut where both will receive instruction in the arts of love by the old guardians. The *mwali*'s ordeal will come to an end when the bridegroom is able to present the full dowry to her family or, again, if the girl gets pregnant. But if the suitor is not satisfied with the girl's behavior, finds her still lazy, unfriendly or uncooperative, he can demand that she stay confined for another year or so, or at least until she is more accommodating. One can imagine the *mwali*'s dependence upon her fiance and how anxious she will be to please him, her relief when he finds her satisfactory, and her happiness when finally allowed to leave the dark hut and join her family in the daylight. Her grateful devotion towards her liberator would make any young man feel like a hero and establish him as her master once and forever.

I often wondered how these adolescent girls, still half children, were able to endure this mental and physical ordeal without sooner or later suffering a nervous breakdown. Mothers sometimes admitted to me that a daughter had died during the time of being a *mwali,* either from a known illness or from no apparent cause. Most *mwali* have to suffer through times of illness without medical help. Only on rare occasions and if a hospital or a physician was not further away than one night's march, would she be allowed to receive medical treatment. If the hospital staff do not know the custom or are not sensitive enough to afford the *mwali* the necessary privacy in the hospital, the family will take her out of the hospital before sunrise, even if the girl is seriously ill. If the *mwali* is not isolated from the other patients, her family has to take the full responsibility for whatever goes wrong with anybody who happened to see the girl.

No wonder, therefore, that I became very popular as physician for the *mwali.* Since I was a woman, there were no objections to letting me into her compound as long as I adapted myself to certain restrictions. I would hardly ever be allowed to stay alone with a *mwali* and questions had to be directed first to the old women who would then relay them to the girl. Usually she sat upon a mat on the floor with her eyes downcast. She whispered her complaints into the ear of one of the old ladies, who then told me. The *mwali* never dared to look at me but kept her eyes firmly shut when I examined her. In pain, she would only whimper, never cry out loudly, and I became amazed at the amount of pain a *mwali* could endure. When I thought they trusted me, I would ask the old women to leave me alone with the girl, and although they usually turned a deaf ear to my request, it sometimes happened that they went out for a little while. Then the *mwali* would look at me, and if I smiled at her, she would smile back with an absorbing intensity and curiosity in her gaze. One sensed her mind's hunger for new impressions. I knew then that whatever I said, the way I looked, the expression on my face, my clothes, my instruments, and the touch of my hands would be remembered in the smallest detail over and over again during lonely hours ahead. The mental craving of these deprived girls must make them extremely suggestible for whatever teaching they receive! Carefully and with as few words as possible I would ask the girl why she so patiently endured this long ordeal as a *mwali*. The girl inevitably looked surprised. Did I not know that without having been a *mwali* a woman would be sterile? And even if she should happen to get pregnant some disaster would befall her. Each *mwali* knew some young woman who had died in childbirth or lost her first child. The reason given was always that the girl had not stuck out her time of confinement, or had rebelled altogether against being a *mwali*.

Sometimes when I was working at a dispensary it happened that a *mwali* was brought there to see me. Her guardians had led her on lonely paths through the thickest bush to avoid meeting other people. They would arrive with her in the evening toward closing time. The little boys who were always hanging around at the dispensary would become excited and whisper to me, "A *mwali* is coming, they are bringing a *mwali!*" People always withdrew to a respectful distance as the *mwali* approached. There was an air of mystery around that deeply veiled figure who walked slowly with head bent, taking care not to show her face lest anybody be harmed by the power of her glance. The little boys walked stiffly up to her and showed their courage by trying to catch a glimpse of the face between the blankets. If they got too close, the guardians chased them away with harsh words. People who otherwise fought for their place in the waiting line, immediately cleared the treatment room when the *mwali* entered and never begrudged the time I spent with her. A feeling of happiness and excitement filled the place; people looked up to a *mwali*. They shared with her the conviction that a woman who did not faithfully go through this period of transition would become infertile and bring bad luck to the whole family because she would be a failure as mother and wife. Therefore people loved the girls who took upon themselves the sacrifice of being a *mwali.* There was a deeply felt sentiment that the preservation of the tribe depended on everybody doing the right thing by living according to ancient teaching and custom.

12
Fanya Bidii: Childbirth in the Bush

Giving birth to her first child is a major milestone in a woman's life. It is the great trial which will decide whether she is to live or die. While working among the tribes of the Ulanga district, I was astonished at the indifference people displayed toward a woman who did not recover from childbirth. It seemed to me that there was not much regret shown for a young woman who perishes in childbirth or much sympathy for her if she could not deliver a healthy baby. In the opinion of the people, the mother herself is to blame for whatever goes wrong during the first pregnancy. I would find such a woman lying neglected in a dark corner of her hut, covered with filth and blood, with only dogs and flies cleaning her infected wounds. Often I came too late, either because nobody had bothered to get help or because the village was too remote and I would see the patient only because I happened to pass through. Sometimes the expecting woman would try to seek help at a mission dispensary or at the Ifakara hospital, traveling if necessary for days through the bush. Some never made it and had to give birth on the way. Puerperal fever, a retained and infected placenta, or severe blood loss and physical exhaustion were often the cause of death. No wonder women approached their first childbirth with apprehension and fear, and that there were numerous taboos and rules to protect and guide them to a safe delivery.

Although I had gathered experience in obstetrics both at hospitals and with midwives in outpost missions, I dreaded being called out to a village to help a woman in labor. The dark huts, uncomfortable and narrow, are ill-suited for childbirth. During the long hours in the dark I often wondered with a sigh why labor pains always have to come on at night and why most babies are born in the early morning hours. It is a myth that African mothers deliver babies easily, especially those living in rural tropical regions. Undernourished and infested with intestinal parasites as they are, they are often poorly developed, with a narrow pelvis and frail physical health. Their anemic condition makes even small post-partum bleeding life-threatening. Old women who have successfully given birth to many children take the lead during delivery and at first I found it very frustrating to cope with them. They talked a lot and tried to interfere with my obstetrical practice, and I used to demand that they leave the hut if I was to take over. But with time I learned that it was better not to provoke these powerful women's wrath by excluding them, since their goodwill was essential for both the young mother and her newborn child. I came to fear them myself too, for when excluded they had plenty of time to set in circulation the wildest speculations about what was happening inside the birth hut. This could be most unpleasant when delivery was not progressing smoothly. There was one event in a village far away from any hospital, which taught me much about the interaction between the expecting mother and her old women helpers. Their behavior towards the woman in labor appeared very strange to me at the time, but I soon found out that they were only acting according to custom.

I had just arrived at Ruaha after a day-long journey by landrover from the Mahenge mission of Kwiro. It was already late and I did not expect to start working before the next day and was looking forward to a good meal in the cool dining room of the mission. But I did not even have time to change or to refresh myself before there was a knock at the door. The priest brought me a trembling young man and asked if I would please help this man's young wife who was in labor. Things were not going well and she was bleeding from the nose, the young man said. That was an unusual place for a childbearing woman to bleed, so I felt alarmed myself. The man assured me that his village was close to the mission, so I took along what I needed for delivery and went with him. As we hurried up and down the hills, through the bush, over streams and far into the forest, I cursed myself for having believed him so readily; people wanting help fast always insisted that they lived "not far away." I had not eaten anything since the morning and my tongue was glued to my gums from thirst. But I consoled myself thinking that someone from the mission would bring me refreshments if I stayed away for a long time, since everybody knew that I could not drink unprepared water or eat indigenous food because of the ubiquitous typhoid fever.

The sun had set before we finally reached the little village half-way between Ruaha and Sali. As we crossed the village square women flocked to me, thanking me for coming to help one of them in her hours of trial. They made some remarks indicating that they expected difficulties for the woman in labor. She had not been a good *mwali*. I understood that there had been some irregularities in her behavior during pregnancy, and I had the feeling that the general attitude towards the expecting mother was rather negative. I found the woman in labor frightened and extremely upset. She was only a girl, fifteen years of age at the most. I looked at her frail body, narrow hips and huge abdomen, and felt the same apprehension as the women outside. She had fresh bruises on her chest and arms; her dry lips were also badly bruised and blood trickled from her swollen nose. "You have beaten her," I exclaimed. The husband avoided my indignant look. He bowed his head and muttered, "Yes, *Mama Mganga,* it was necessary; she is lazy, she will not do her work."

103

The room was crowded. A bunch of old women huddled together on a bed, while the expecting mother lay on the ground and pushed herself against the wall as if in self-defence. The old ladies were agitated and quite intimidating. I felt it too. "She is lazy!" They hurled out the accusation. "She will not *fanya bidii!*" I had often heard this expression used for a woman in labor. It can best be translated as "be courageous; take pains; work hard; pull yourself together." The old women were gesticulating and talking all at once when suddenly the bed broke down under their weight and they tumbled onto the floor. With their arms and feet thrashing around they looked much like old crows in their dark clothes. I had to suppress a sudden impulse to laugh and used the moment of embarrassment to demand that everybody leave the room except for the girl's mother and a few others. We then restored the bed as best we could and assisted the girl to lay down on it. The bed was still out of shape and slanted to one side; but it was better than having the woman in labor lying naked on the dirt floor. The girl's mother brought forth a coconut she had saved for this event, cut it open, and asked me to wash my fingers in the clear fluid so that I could examine the girl internally.

The East African tribes among whom I worked had the unfortunate custom of making the woman bear down as soon as the first labor pains start. From that moment on, until the baby is born, she is not given anything to eat or drink or else they think the child will fall asleep and not try to find its way out. The ill-effects of this are two-fold. Being pushed downward before the mouth of the womb is open, the child's head presses on the half-opened muscular ring, causing the tissue to swell and not retract properly. Birth is therefore prolonged unnecessarily, even for days, and all the strength of the woman is drained. Because the hard-laboring woman has had nothing to drink or eat, she will be utterly exhausted before the final stage of birth sets in when she needs all her physical powers to expel the baby.

As I carefully palpated the womb of this young girl, I

could feel the swollen muscular ring of the cervix. It was far from being wide enough to allow the baby to descend and delivery could not possibly proceed, even if the old women had all beaten her and forced her to *fanya bidii*. I placed her on her back with her legs elevated to get the pressure off the swollen tissue, gave her a pain killing injection, and in spite of the mother's protest, made her drink some water in which I had mixed sugar and vitamins. I then cleaned her wounds and put a moist cloth on her bleeding nose whilst I talked friendly to the terrified girl until she relaxed and dozed off. We all waited in the dark little room where a small fire on the floor gave the only light. I was hungry and thirsty and worried. The girl had very pale conjunctivae, a sure sign of anemia. Her arms and legs were skinny and all nourishment appeared to have gone into the child which seemed grotesquely large in her abdomen. Delivery would certainly be hard and very painful. Outside we could hear the old ladies debating angrily. I could have walked back to the mission to get some food for myself and still be back in time, but I did not dare to leave the young mother, lest her folks should beat her up again.

We were aroused by the girl's loud cry. Labor was setting in with renewed force after the pause. Mother placed herself behind the girl, took her daughter between her own legs and put her arms around the swollen abdomen. The others held the girl's legs apart and I knelt beside her. Each time the pains came on I made the women stroke the girl's arms and legs, massage her back and press her hands. Between contractions I let her walk. We talked to her and assured the frightened girl that everything was all right. It helped, and when the right time came, she clenched her teeth and bore down with all her might. Sweat poured down her body and the child seemed to rise up inside the womb, but all to no avail. The child's head seemed to be stuck in the narrow bony passage. Hour after hour we sat with her whilst waves of pain passed through her body. One could see the child move under the tight skin. The girl's moans and groans rose to long tortured wails.

Outside it was dark. Why did nobody come from the

mission? I desperately needed some refreshment. At times my feelings of thirst were stronger than my concern for the woman in labor. My stomach was hollow and ached from hunger, the smoke from the fire burned in my eyes, the night was hot and the air heavy; it seemed to go on forever. At times the girl was in my arms. I looked down at the sweet childlike face, now swollen and contorted from the struggle. She trusted me, but I felt faint and could hardly find the strength to hold her up. The contractions became increasingly powerful. It seemed incredible that this frail girl had so much strength, but she was fighting for her life and for the life of her child. Restraining my wish to quench my thirst with the rest of the coconut milk, I again wet my fingers and examined the girl. The mouth of the womb was swollen and still not fully opened. During the next few labor pains I forcibly widened the opening with my finger. Blood trickled from the wounded tissue and the girl screamed in pain. "Enough, *Mama Mganga,*" she whispered, pleadingly in between the pains. I was sweating too and felt nervous. What if she was hemorrhaging to death? But something had to be done to make birth progress; the girl did not seem to have much strength left. Between the pains, her eyes rolled upwards and I thought she was unconscious. Her mother and the others also became increasingly anxious. Death seemed to lurk somewhere in the dark.

I felt lonely, weak and scared. What a difference it was, I thought, conducting delivery in the safety of a clean hospital with nurses and colleagues ready to help. Even death appears less frightening when one has all the devices of modern medicine around and knows that everything possible is being done. But here in the dirty, dark, windowless hut, smoky and hot, surrounded by scared and apprehensive women, hungry and thirsty, with the burden of responsibility on my shoulders alone, it was another story. "I am dying," the girl gasped after an exhausting futile series of contractions. It was essential that she did not give up. Only her own strength, especially her mental strength, would help her ward off death now. Her moral strength, her tolerance for pain, her willingness to endure, her love for her family and her sense of duty would help her overcome the hardships facing her in this situation. Maybe that was what custom taught the girls during the confinement in puberty when they as *mwali* were shown that life for a woman is no fun there in the African bush, and that only by *fanya bidii* can they be prepared for the even harder ordeal of giving birth to their first child. I looked at this girl not yet fully developed for the task of giving birth. Being a *mwali,* closed up in a compound, protects a girl from getting pregnant too early, I thought, and remembered that the women in the village had indicated that this girl had not gone through her *mwali* period properly. Maybe there was more wisdom in their customs than I had thought.

Another violent contraction wrenched the girl from her semiconscious condition. She wailed and worked and struggled but could not get the baby to move down. I placed her on the edge of the bed with her legs hanging down, a position which sometimes helps when the baby's head is stuck in the bony passage but she could not endure that position for very long. I tried to remember other maneuvers. When the next pains came on, I had her hold on to the ceiling and hang down, but she dropped into our laps. Then the mother and her helpers turned against me: what good did I do? What use was there in my medicine? Why could I not make the child be born? The mother spat on the floor in disgust. Anger surged through me—as if I had not suffered with them through the night! "Alright, then, I will leave," I said and stood up. I felt a sudden relief, seeing before me my bed in the cool quiet room at the mission where everything was right: no pains, no sweating, no screaming and wailing, no blood and dirt. I reached the opening of the hut, the cool fresh air struck my face, and without thinking of the impossible long way through the dark I was just going to slip out when I felt my leg seized from behind. "Please *Mama Mganga,* don't leave me, oh don't forsake me or I must die." The girl held me back, sobs shook her body and her bloodshot eyes looked at me in despair. Of course I could not leave her. I turned and sat down again by the fire. My head was spinning and for a moment it was black before my eyes. I felt utterly powerless.

Just to do something and to give her and myself a break from the choking atmosphere in the hut, I made her come outside. The poor girl could hardly crawl, but she breathed in the fresh air with some relief. Then another pain threw her to the ground. She gave a wild shriek and all the old women who had been lingering around in the dark came to life. They rushed past me, seized the screaming girl and carried her into the hut. Now they took over; they seemed to know what to do. One took out of her cloth some white dye and painted a stripe across the girl's abdomen from the navel down to the pubic region for the baby to see its way. Others clapped their hands in front of the birth opening for the child to hear where to get out. When this did not help they sent for the men. The young husband who seemed out of his wits for fear was placed at the moaning woman's side and her father behind her back. He took her head on his lap, bent down over her sweating face and asked with a stern voice, "Who did you fool around with during the time of your pregnancy?" The girl gave him a scared look, then she glanced at her husband and at the other men around her. She whimpered, "I did not fool around with anybody." She noticed the anger and disapproval on all their faces. A contraction interrupted the inquest. The old women slapped her full in the face when she gave in and screamed out in her pain. "*Fanya bidii, haya! Fanya bidii,*" they all shouted in a chorus and showed her how to bear down. They came in sweat themselves. It helped for a while.

In between the pains the father hovered over her urging her to name the adulterer who was causing her not to be able to give birth. It was obvious to everybody, he said, that she must have done something wrong. He told her to whisper the name into his ear if she did not want the others to hear, and he pinched her painfully to underline his words. But the girl only wept. Now she had lost all her courage and gave up completely. When the next contraction seized her she screamed

108

and screamed and the continued over-breathing took away the effect of labor. The peoples' agitation was rising to a pitch. Suddenly they all jumped upon the girl. I was pushed aside and forceful hands closed around her nose and mouth, fists and feet stamped and pounded and kicked her body. I saw only arms and feet and flying clothes as the girl struggled to get her breath, giving out some awful sounds. Dust was whirled up, embers from the fire flew around and burned the clothes, a little boy who had slept in a corner started to scream, hens fluttered up in the air and rushed out of the hut. Just as I thought they had choked the girl to death the baby's head broke through. In the midst of the terrible confusion I tried to get hold of the head, but it was smeared with blood and slipped out of my hands. I shouted at the people who continued to pound the poor girl. Between hands and feet and sweating bodies I finally grasped the head and pulled at it. The girl writhed and gave a last terrifying scream, blood poured over my hands, but the baby was born.

It had a badly deformed head and there was no sign of life in it but I hurriedly cut the umbilical cord, took the slimy little thing and rushed out with it, remembering that there was a little stream behind the hut. There I dipped the limp body in the cold water, slapped its back and tried the usual manipulations to force out the first cry. But there was no sound; the baby did not breathe and I was just going to examine it closer when the old ladies came out of the hut. They looked around alarmed, and when they saw me with the baby, they ran towards me and one of them snatched the lifeless body out of my hands. I wanted it back. "Quickly, give it back to me, every minute counts, I must make the baby breathe." I took a step towards them, but they looked so threatening and agitated that I stopped. What was the matter? Why this sudden hostility? I sensed danger for my own life. "The baby is dead, there is nothing *you* can do, it belongs to us." It was the oldest woman speaking harshly to me. "This girl is no good and you have no right to the child's body." She turned her back on me, wrapped the dead baby in a cloth with angry movements and marched off into the forest. Much later I learned that a still-born baby is a very powerful item for use in witchcraft. Evidently the apprehensive old women I had barred from the hut during the delivery figured that I wanted the dead baby for black magic purposes.

Bewildered and dazed I returned to the hut to look after the girl. She was now crying softly. "My baby, I want my baby," she whispered over and over again, ignoring the others who treated her with contempt. "What a useless woman you are," they said. "The child is dead, it was all to no avail." The girl was bleeding badly and her abdomen seemed just as big as before. Still shaky from the confrontation with the hostile old women, I felt fear in this situation. If the girl died, what would happen to me so far away from the mission, alone with these suspicious people? I decided to remove the placenta manually in order to stop the deadly bleeding. Nobody seemed interested in what I did any more so I placed one hand on the girl's abdomen and with the other I felt my way through the torn tissues. Then my hand touched something like a little foot. I was electrified. Another baby! It had to come out quickly or the girl would certainly perish. She could not possibly give birth to another child. All my senses fully alert, I carefully slid my hand along the baby's body until I felt the groove of the neck, then feeling the chin I got my index finger into its mouth and with the guiding help of my outer hand I slowly turned the child around. Fortunately no contraction closed the womb around the child's body, which would have made the operation much more difficult. As it was, the womb was wide and with a little force I could guide the baby through the open birth-canal. It came out together with the after-birth and another gush of blood. The girl let out a yell; everybody turned to her and to their amazement saw me hold up a baby girl. It curled up its legs and sounded the well-known cry of a healthy newborn baby.

All the tension, hostility and unhappiness from before melted away. The women wept and laughed with joy, clapped their hands and caressed the new mother. They grasped my

110

hands and thanked me as if I had conjured up the second child. Nobody had thought of the possibility that the pregnant girl might have twins. That was why she had had such a huge abdomen. The contractions of the over-extended muscle fibres of a womb holding twins are less effective than when there is only one child—one certain reason for difficult labor. The people in the bush, who believe that the placenta is another baby, deformed and therefore dead, see no difference between an after-birth and a stillborn baby; thus the same old lady now received the "real" placenta from my hands, wrapped it in another cloth and went out to bury it under a certain tree together with the stillborn baby from before. Eager hands now lit the scattered fire and prepared some food for the exhausted young mother. The uterus had meanwhile contracted to form a hard lump in her abdomen. There was no more bleeding, but I gave her a shot of a large dose of penicillin to prevent puerperal fever. The girl slept peacefully with a happy smile on her face. Now that she had produced a living child she had nothing more to fear.

I walked down to the river with aching limbs. It was already morning. People looked at me and laughed as I wearily washed off the worst dirt from the long struggle. As I stood there on the bank of the little river I felt I was going to faint. I quickly sat down. The people at the mission obviously had forgotten all about me and I knew I could not possibly walk back to the mission without some kind of refreshment. When I had recovered a little I asked for some cooked rice and chicken, thinking that when newly cooked it could not harm me. The women gladly complied and looked on amused while I ate what seemed to me the best meal I had ever eaten. The young husband appeared with a bicycle. Would *Mama Mganga* sit on the back while he cycled to the mission? He seemed embarrassed, maybe because of the way they had treated me. I was happy to leave and although it was an uncomfortable way of traveling, I was glad I did not have to walk the whole way back. The waters of the rivers we had to wade across woke me up, and when we reached the mission where

111

everybody was still asleep, I felt refreshed and exhilarated. Stretching out on my bed, I felt that I had learned something.

To be born and to die in a natural way are processes which take time, I thought. Birth and death are painful and in many ways alike. Few are those who are well prepared for the agony of either. Once the process has started, there is no way back. Dying leads to death, and giving birth to the border of death "*Ninakufa*—I am dying." Each woman I had helped in childbirth said these words at one point in her delivery. Some did die, but most found the strength to *fanya bidii;* they overcome death by giving life to a new human being.

13
The Devil's Dance

Theresia was brought to me in Kwiro by a group of neighbor women. They had her in their midst, supporting her around the waist and holding her by her arms. They looked worried and angry, while Theresia was trembling and sobbing and gasping for air. As soon as her friends let her go she sank to the floor. Choking spells forced her to sit up and she rubbed her neck and rocked her body, whining pitifully between the sobs. Sweat and tears poured down her face. Her clothes were torn and she was covered with dirt as if she had been rolling on the ground. I led her to our emergency room and helped her on to the bed. Her body was shaking so violently I could not examine her properly. Her heart was pounding wildly, she had bruises, and blood was trickling from cuts and scratches. I washed her trembling body, put cooling compresses on the bruises and tried to find out what had happened. But she was completely absorbed in her own misery; she did not even hear me. Her heartbreaking sobbing and crying seemed to express just as much mental as physical hurt. Touched by her profound unhappiness, I stayed with her, hoping that if words could not help, my presence might comfort her in some way.

It was a shock for me to see a woman so utterly unable to control herself. I had learned to admire the women of the mountain people among whom I was working; they had a great capability to remain strong and calm in the face of tragedy. There always seemed to be plenty of worry and misfortune in their lives: a sick child, death of a loved one, ailing parents, an abusive husband, not enough food to keep above starvation. And yet, the women were always ready to smile and laugh; they took advantage of any opportunity to enjoy themselves and to make those around them happy. The women worked hard day in and day out the year round. Work might change with the seasons, but it never ended. The family's well-being depended upon the woman's capacity for labor. I had seen women at work in the fields, a baby on their back and another child hanging in a sling on their hip. Why not put down the child? There were venomous insects, snakes and wild animals in the grass, too dangerous for little children who could not yet stand upright or run. If the mother was lucky, one of her daughters would be old enough to take the child on her little back for a while. The women were courageous and somehow they possessed the stamina to overcome the drudgery of their daily toiling, knowing instinctively that they had to fight physical weakness, pain and tiredness in order to keep going and that their families' survival depended on their endurance.

One of the women's daily tasks was to grind flour in big wooden mortars with heavy poles. A strong back and strong arms were needed for this work. "She cannot pound maize any more," was a standing expression for someone wanting to tell me that a woman was very ill, and "she has picked up the pounding pole again," indicated that she had recovered. Sometimes a woman would neglect herself, or not find time to get treatment for the ubiquitous parasitic infestations, and then she would grow too weak even to walk. I have seen such women dragging themselves to the dispensary, their babies still on their backs, faces and limbs swollen from severe anemia and their blood looking like water when drawn from their fingers for testing. I marveled at their ability to recover under medical treatment and often thought they got well through sheer will power. They seemed to have this urge to survive in order to protect their children. When seriously ill they would anxiously ask, "How will my family survive? What will happen to my children if I die?" The people did not know any other ways of feeding babies and little children than by mother's milk but due to complicated rules and taboos of the Wapogoro people it was impossible for another woman to offer her milk to the child of a deceased mother. Therefore, if a mother died, her small children would perish with her. The older children able to walk would find food and shelter with relatives and might survive.

Mothers, well aware of the danger for their little ones, were careful to avoid another pregnancy until their baby was old enough to eat ordinary food. That meant sexual abstinence for at least two years, during which time they accepted that the husband might turn to other women. Traditionally the husband could take a second or third wife, and quite a few women I spoke with preferred this solution to having their husband fooling around. I once gave a necklace to a village chief for his wife as thanks for some services he had rendered but he looked embarrassed and did not want to accept the gift. He asked me to wait and went home to return with three laughing women, all young and handsome. "Which of them should I give the necklace? They are all my wives," he said proudly. I came to know his three wives quite well and learned how they managed to get along in their daily life. They were like sisters to each other, and although each of them had her own hut, they coordinated their work. Pooling their children, one of the wives looked after all of them while the other two were free to work in the fields or attend to some other task. At times the chief took one of his wives on his many trips, making sure they all had their turn. How he successfully divided his affection between them I do not know, but he seemed to keep them happy. Few men, however, were wealthy or strong enough to manage more than one wife.

Generally women showed great tolerance toward their husbands. The teaching they received during their seclusion period prepared them well for a subservient role in marriage, and social rules and customs upheld and fortified male superiority. A woman was supposed to walk a few steps behind the husband, carrying heavy loads while he might not carry anything but his walking stick. During meals the husband was to be served first and to receive the best and biggest morsels. When men spoke, women were to keep quiet and look down. They were supposed to listen and to respect men's wishes. Mothers seemed to have a peculiar respect for their male children too. I never saw a mother impatient with her child or letting it cry unattended. If a little boy was disobedient, his mother would patiently persuade him until he went along; if he hit her in anger she would protect herself with a forgiving smile. Once when a boy struck out at his mother rather viciously I asked her why she did not reprimand the child? A good smack on the behind would put him in his place, I said. She was startled. "Oh no, how could I!" she exclaimed. "Don't you know that our forefathers' spirits are reborn in our children? What if this boy is my reborn grandfather? How could you spank your own grandparent?"

I looked at Theresia as I sat with her in the little room. She was still crying. I spoke to her again and she grabbed my arm with her trembling hands. "I got the Devil in my neck." She twisted her body. "He is pushing me down," she muttered with chattering teeth. Her face was swollen from crying so long. "*Shetani,* the Devil is choking me, I'll die," she gasped. Shaking and sobbing overwhelmed her again. Was there nothing I could do to comfort her? Rarely had I seen a woman so downcast. Even when standing in line with their sick children, waiting anxiously for treatment at the dispensary, the women would quickly cheer each other up. With shiny teeth flashing between their smiling lips, they would joke and laugh, drawing from a well of warmth and strength that never seemed to dry up. Women readily helped each other when in trouble and neighbors would always know and sympathize if a wife had marital problems. Such difficulties were taken seriously and well-meaning intervention by the neighbors was always at hand. If this did not improve the situation, the woman might return to her parents for a while. Great pressure would be exerted to make her conform, for if her husband refused to take her back, her parents would have to return the bridal price to him and keep the daughter. As in all human societies there were unhappy marriages and family quarrels in spite of everybody's efforts to help the couple to get along. Wife beating was not uncommon, and if it did not happen too often, it was tolerated by the woman. I suspected that Theresia had been beaten, perhaps just once too often. She certainly appeared at her wits' end. Maybe she would calm down if left alone. I finally went outside to ask the neighbor women what had happened to her.

Theresia's brother had joined the indignant group of women. He was angry and insisted he should be the one telling me what was the matter. But they all talked at once and it was difficult to sort out the facts from the angry accusations against her husband. I gathered that Theresia was one of many children of a village headman. When the children were small their father had lived in peace with his four wives. But when Theresia was seven years old the two youngest wives decided to leave the old man. To Theresia's chagrin her mother moved in with a young man and during the family quarrels that followed, she was sent off to a boarding school for girls, run by the mission. At the age of fourteen her family married her off to an old man who died while she was still at school. She had to spend two boring years in mourning until she was betrothed again. This time she suffered under a brutal man who beat her severely. Under these circumstances custom permitted her to seek refuge at her father's place. Her family refunded the bridal money and Theresia stayed at her parental home with her only child. She was now free to marry again. It was during this time that she met the man she had now been living with for the last fifteen years. They had three children.

Theresia was very fond of this man and made all kinds of

excuses for him for not paying her family the full bridal price but this caused permanent friction between the two families. To live with a man who considered her not worth the full bridal price was looked upon as a disgrace for any woman. Theresia, however, appeared to be happy until about a year ago when her husband inherited the young wife of his deceased brother. From then on he began to criticize Theresia; he was impatient with her and favored the other woman. Theresia felt very threatened by the presence of the younger woman and by the fact that the husband began to beat her much in the same way as her first husband had done. Neighbors would find her standing alone behind the house, staring at the mountains with a sad and forlorn expression on her face. Theresia's older brother, now the head of the family, was annoyed at the treatment his sister had to endure. He insisted that the husband pay him the full bridal price for Theresia, but the husband refused and the two men had many quarrels about the matter until finally the husband angrily shouted he did not want Theresia anyhow; nothing would please him more than to see her return to her family. Theresia felt caught between the two. She did not at all want to leave her husband, but she knew that her brother had the right to take her back. He could get her married again and in that way procure the bridal price her husband refused to pay. She felt deeply hurt and rejected and was afraid her husband would indeed send her away. However, he could make true his threats only as long as she was well. Custom demands that a husband has to keep his sick wife, and Theresia felt sick. She began to have shaking spells and complained of having bad heart pain. This made her husband even more irritable towards her and he continued to mistreat her. When he again gave her a beating without any justifiable reason, Theresia could not take it any more. The neighbors heard her crying for hours and when the women went over to her place they found her lying on the ground just as the husband had left her, bruised and hurt. She did not respond to their efforts to console her so they brought her to the dispensary.

118

In the days that followed, Theresia refused to leave the room. She would not eat and continued to cry for hours, causing much consternation to her neighbors and friends. She refused to see her husband and I had the impression that Theresia was determined to make him change his attitude. She continued to be extremely depressed and to talk about the Devil torturing her. Again neighbors and relatives assembled outside the room where Theresia was staying. Her brother and husband were also present, and when Theresia finally came out to join them, their arguing became excited. The sullen husband and angry brother again started one of their usual quarrels when suddenly Theresia uttered a loud cry and dropped to the ground. She began to breathe laboriously and her eyes widened in fear as she lifted her head and stared at some invisible horror in front of her. "Help, help, *Shetani,* the Devil is grabbing me!" she yelled and threw herself on her back with jerking arms and legs as if fighting with the Devil. Then she jumped up and ran off, gesticulating and shouting, tearing off her clothes in the struggle until she disappeared naked in the bush. Two women immediately set out after her. Everybody was stunned by the dramatic scene. The women turned to the now fearful looking husband. "You are a fine one," they scolded him, "mistreating Theresia in such a way! Now she is possessed by *Shetani* and will perish somewhere in the bush if we don't succeed in catching her, subduing her and bringing her back." The presence of *Shetani* was a threat to the whole village, they continued, and only the joint efforts of all the women could prevent further tragedy. They would now have to perform a Devil's dance; *ngoma ya Shetani.* It would be hard work for the women, they would have to perform rituals and dances until *Shetani* was forced to name the conditions upon which he would let go of Theresia and disappear from the village. Angrily the women turned away from the men and walking homewards they loudly discussed their plans; behind them followed the intimidated husband and brother.

Having decided to hold a *ngoma ya Shetani,* the women set out to prepare the ritual. Theresia was found in the bush and put in isolation, waiting for the ceremony to begin. From now on the women appeared to be in a state of continued agitation. They shouted instead of talking as they ran around gathering firewood and preparing food for the days to come. The small hand drums used in the ceremony were taken from storage and repaired. New ones were made and dyes were mixed for the decoration of their bodies during the dance. The men kept wisely out of the way and the children were sent off to relatives in other villages. I inquired whether I would be allowed to attend the dance, but every woman I asked declined. The *ngoma ya Shetani* was a dangerous matter, they said, and no stranger had ever been allowed to see it. Outsiders also warned me; some because they believed the Devil to be indeed present at this ritual; others because they thought the women could be quite dangerous when working themselves into the frenzy required for the ceremony. Everybody at the mission made arrangements to stay away from the village and not to get anywhere close to the place where the *ngoma ya Shetani* was to be performed.

One evening when I opened my door I heard faint drumming from the direction of the village. I listened into the dark. It was not the usual drumbeats I knew so well from many feasts. This was a very rapid rhythm—an eerie sound which made my heart beat faster. I knew the *ngoma ya Shetani* had begun. I had been told that no woman could withstand the calling of these drums. Even far away, where nobody else could hear it, women would perceive the fast beats. Unable to resist, as if drawn by a magnet, they would drop whatever they were doing and run through bush and fields until they reached the village where the *ngoma ya Shetani* was taking place. An intense curiosity made me forget all warnings. I turned off the lights in my room, locked the door and slipped away from the mission, following a path in the direction of the calling drums. I strained my eyes in the dark and proceeded very slowly hiding each time I heard the quick footsteps of a woman running behind me. I held my breath as the dim figures whisked past me in the dark and a feeling of unreality gripped me. It was as if I had been placed in a scene right out of the medieval Walpurgis Night with witches scurrying off to their Sabbath. I sneaked ever closer with pounding heart until I could hear the crackling of the fire and the excited voices of many women. Not daring to approach any further, I found a place where I could hide in the bush.

From my hideout I could faintly feel the heat of the huge blaze, and see the silhouettes of women running in front of the fire. At one side I could distinguish a person sitting in a stooped position completely covered by a blanket. That must be Theresia, I thought. More and more women arrived. They began to arrange themselves in a circle and to dance around the fire holding on to each other and singing in unison. Some of them were beating their small hand drums and as they danced the rhythm became faster and faster. Dust was stirred up and dimmed the view. The women looked like ghosts as they began to break away from the circle and whirl around on their own in an ever quicker tempo. Shrieks and angry cries interrupted the singing and the air seemed charged with aggression as the women worked themselves into a frenzy. Woe to the man who would dare to come within sight of these furies! I could fully believe what I had been told, that the raging women would fall upon a male intruder and beat him senseless or even kill him. Nobody could blame them afterwards since they were possessed and had therefore lost control of their actions. It seemed to me that the *ngoma ya Shetani* was a female outcry, a protest against male dominance. Maybe this was the only time women could act out their frustration and their pent-up resentment against men. No wonder men kept silent and hid in their huts during the time the *Shetani* was around. I could imagine the grudge the men would have against the unwise husband who had unleashed these evil forces in their village.

From my hiding place I saw one dancing figure after the other clutching the drum and beating away in a fantastically rapid rhythm, thereby igniting the others to an ever-increasing ecstasy. From time to time one of them would be flung to the

121

ground, throwing her arms and legs around, grappling much in the same way as Theresia had done when she announced the *Shetani* was upon her. Clothes were flying and the smell of singed fabric was in my nose. Suddenly the drumming stopped and the women tumbled to one side of the fire. A few of them started to dance towards the covered figure which I thought was Theresia. They beat their drums again and danced around her and slowly the person under the blanket began to move. As the drumming intensified the women moved faster, making stroking movements over the crouching figure. The blanket fluttered but was not thrown off. I could not see the woman underneath and from a distance it looked as if the blanket was hovering above the ground, moving swiftly in the air in rhythm with the drums. It appeared to be a living being in itself, a grotesque blanket-being! The whole thing looked very spooky to me and I suddenly feared some of the women in their altered state of mind might perceive my presence and discover me behind the trees. I was shivering in the cold night and felt it was time for me to retreat. Slowly and cautiously I backed off from the scene and groped my way back to the path. Only then did I dare to walk upright. Not a soul met me on the way back to the mission; even the animals seemed scared away. I could not help smiling when I thought of all the brave men huddling in their huts anxiously listening to the noise, imagining their women-folk dancing out there with the Devil! I was sure that the memory of such a demoniac orgy would help keep the men in line and warn them not to misuse the right they had over women.

The *ngoma ya Shetani* continued for three days and four nights. Finally the women, exhausted and still angry, summoned all the men to a meeting. The leader of the dancers announced in front of all the villagers that the *Shetani* would leave Theresia and the village on the condition that her husband give a new garment to his wife and pay her brother the full bridal price. The *Shetani* threatened to return and possess Theresia again should the husband continue to mistreat her. Grudgingly the husband consented to the Devil's demands.

He knew that having exposed his fellow men to the risks and embarrassment of a *ngoma ya Shetani* he could not afford to refuse or else they might well chase him away from the village. He actually had no choice but to pay everything and take better care of Theresia lest the Devil should plague them again. But that was not all. He also had to pay off all the women who had "worked" so hard to cure his wife of her possession and who had with so much effort obliged the Devil to leave the village. Thus the *ngoma ya Shetani* had helped to restore the equilibrium of power between male and female and to re-establish peace between husband and wife.

14
Susanna the Teacher and her Liberation

One of the windows in my room at the Kwiro mission faced the court yard of the boarding school which housed about two hundred high school girls from the Mahenge mountain district. The girls slept in large dormitories and most of their daily off-school activities were performed in this spacious yard where a group of large mango trees gave cooling shade in the heat of the mid-day sun. I loved the gay noises when the girls swarmed out into the yard after school and could watch them washing clothes in long heavy basins in one corner of the yard, hanging their laundry in the sun on drying racks outside their living quarters. Some girls sifted grain and spread corn on mats to dry; others pounded maize under the trees. Many girls merely amused themselves playing ball or stood in small groups chatting and laughing together.

The solid brick structures of the school surrounded the yard and all doors faced inwards so that the whole compound was completely closed off from the outside world. Only one narrow gate led out, and that gate was just outside my room. Every morning I was awakened by the girls filing past on their way to church for the early morning mass. I liked the sound of

124

the many naked feet on the flat stones of the passage and the subdued giggling of the girls. They knew I was there and had a little game with me, coughing or clearing their throats the way they had heard me do it, or tapping lightly at my door as they passed by. Sometimes I opened the door on them and the nearest girls would jump aside startled, while others burst out laughing. I heard them still chuckling as they filed into the church, under the eyes of their stern teachers who were standing at the entrance counting the girls and making sure everybody was present.

Each Saturday afternoon the girls were allowed to have a dance. They would drag their huge drums into the courtyard and take turns at beating them while the other girls were singing and dancing, hands on each others shoulder. I often looked at the girls through my window, enjoying the sight and sounds and thinking that these years spent within the protective walls of the mission school might be the happiest time of their lives.

Except for priests, no man was ever allowed inside the school gate. Any male, even the father or other close relative wanting to visit one of the girls, had to turn to Mother Superior. Upon her approval a meeting would be arranged in a supervised room outside the school. On Sunday after Mass people had a chance to see the girls as they crossed the lawn from church to school. Parents and friends lined the well-trodden path where the girls walked and here boys and young men could look at the girls and sweethearts might exchange a few words or a girl receive a gift from an admirer until a watchful nun or teacher ordered her back into line. Because of this strict control over the girls and their isolation from men, people accepted this boarding school as a proper place for their adolescent daughters. According to the custom of the *mwali,* girls were usually withdrawn from school as soon as they reached puberty and kept in isolation until they were married. But some parents agreed to let their daughters spend their years of seclusion at this particular school because it was so well-guarded. Not only would their daughters remain virgins here, they would learn many skills and the family would

125

be assured of a high bridal price. Besides the usual academic subjects, the girls took courses in modern childrearing, health care, cooking, gardening, sewing and other domestic arts. The high bridal price the families of these girls could demand also secured them prestigious sons-in-law, since only boys from well-to-do families or men with education and well-paid jobs could come up with the necessary sum.

Few girls actually made it to graduation; it was not up to them to decide how long they stayed. While they were living at the school, happy to receive education and to be with other girls instead of sitting alone in a dark hut, their families were busy arranging a match for them. Any day a girl could receive a message from home that she was to be married and had to be prepared for the wedding on a given Sunday. If she was lucky, she would marry her sweetheart; maybe the boy who had made up to her on the way to church, somebody she liked and from whom she therefore had accepted gifts. These marriages were big events for the other girls, who would eagerly help the bride sew her garments and dress her up for the wedding. On the memorable Sunday, before the church ceremony, they would accompany the bride across the school yard, giving the women's characteristic cry of joy. At the gate they would circle around the bride and together they would shed tears as she bade farewell to a carefree girlhood before she stepped out through the gate to begin her life as a woman. Many curious pairs of eyes would mercilessly inspect the bridegroom who awaited the bride on the other side of the gate. Embarrassed, he would clumsily offer his arm as he received her from the girls and lead her to the church. After the service there was another tearful farewell to teachers and girl friends before the couple went on their way to celebrate the wedding at home according to their people's tradition. On Sunday afternoon after such a wedding, the schoolyard was quiet. Maybe the girls were sad because their friend was gone, maybe they whispered to each other about their own dreams and hopes for the future as they sat around in the dormitories.

Most of the teachers at the school were European nuns

126

but there were also a few African nuns who kept house with the girls. They came from the same tribes and acted as house-mothers, helping to overcome the homesickness to which the adolescent girls were prone during the long absence from their families. Only one lay teacher was an African woman. Her name was Susanna and she was very popular. She used to accompany sick girls when they came to the dispensary for treatment and I was astonished at first when I learned that she was a teacher. She did not look much older than some of the schoolgirls but all her colleagues praised her as being unusually diligent. She was a pleasant, quiet person and we had no difficulties communicating since her command of English was indeed very good. I was always happy when she came with the sick girls, for she was an attentive listener and appeared genuinely concerned about her students. She was bright and I knew that she would understand my orders correctly. I often saw her helping the girls in their daily tasks, and wherever she appeared the students would flock together around her. She was a local girl whose family lived in a village not far from the mission, but Susanna seldom went to visit them. Her little room was beside the girls' dormitories and she rarely ever left the mission.

Late one evening I was awakened by a commotion in the girls' dormitories and heard them running about calling for help. I dressed quickly and was ready just in time when somebody knocked at my door. "Please *Mama Mganga,* come quickly, Susanna is ill!" I hurried across the yard. Susanna's little room was crowded. The upset girls rushed around in confusion, some crying for fear. Susanna was on her bed, holding her head with both hands and whimpering, "Oh, oh, my head, my head is bursting, I am dying, call the priest, get holy water, my head is burning, Oh, please, cooling water—here, here, place it on my head. Quick, more water or my head will burst." The girls hurried back and forth dipping pieces of cloth in a water bucket and placing them on Susanna's forehead until both she and the bed were soaking wet. Trembling all over, Susanna clutched the rosary in her hands and begged the priest to give her the last rites. She did not seem to understand when we spoke to her and she held on to us and stuttered for fear: "*Nakufa, nakufa*—I am dying, I am dying." Yet, apart from fast heart beats and sweaty hands, I could find nothing physically wrong with her, and the nurse who by now had joined us agreed that Susanna was merely in a state of panic. The girls who felt more courageous in our presence whispered about *uchavi,* witchcraft. They told us that Susanna had been well as usual when they bade her good night. They woke up when Susanna yelled in the night and jumped out of bed. They heard her crying for help and expressing fear that her uncle had cast a spell on her. We were able to make Susanna swallow a sedative and watched her until she calmed down and finally fell asleep. Some of the girls asked if they could stay with her. They hauled a mattress into the room and lay down close to Susanna's bed, happy to be able to do something for their beloved teacher. The others returned to their dormitories and soon everybody was back to sleep.

When Susanna woke up next morning she was again seized by a feeling of terror. She sent a girl for me and when I arrived at her bedside she pleaded with me not to let her die. She was extremely agitated and did not dare to be left alone. Her pleading sounded so urgent that I was quite alarmed. It was so unlike Susanna. We had all known her as a calm, composed and happy person, not at all prone to hysterics. She must be in great emotional distress, I thought, and made arrangements to stay with her for a while. I sent the girls off to their classrooms and sat down beside the distressed young teacher, asking her to tell me what had happened. She gave a sigh and looked at me with a tense and worried expression. "We are alone, Susanna, nobody will disturb us, do tell me what is bothering you," I tried to coax her. There was a quiver around her mouth and she was evasive. "It's a long story." She closed her eyes. "Please give me some time," she whispered.

I waited patiently. Finally she opened her eyes wide and staring out into space she told me of a dream which had caused her sudden panic the night before. She dreamt that she was walking up a hill with her parents. She had hurried to reach the top before them. But when she stood on the summit looking around, she felt uneasy. It was as if the entire scenery was changing and she sensed danger. Suddenly a lion appeared and her mother and father turned and ran down the hill leaving her in the lurch. She tried to escape but could not move. As the lion jumped at her she woke up with a scream, terrified and convinced she was about to die. She did not recognize where she was and even the trees outside in the yard appeared strange to her; she then cried out for help, sure that it was her uncle who had sent the lion to kill her. Susanna began to tremble again and repeated that it was her fate to perish through her uncle's witchcraft; now he had finally caught up with her. Susanna cried and I felt there was more to it than the dream. "Look Susanna," I tried to persuade her, "tell me all about it, maybe I can help you." She gave me a tearful glance. "Would you really care to hear?" she asked with a timid voice. I took her hand. "Of course I do, I want to help you." She lay still for a while. Then she began:

"When I was a little girl, I had a sister whom I adored. She was older than I and used to carry me around on her back. She was so full of life—it was always fun to be with her. I must have been about seven years old when she had to withdraw for her puberty rites to live as a *mwali* in seclusion. I missed her very much and often tried to visit her. But my father built a high fence of banana leaves around the hut and did not allow me to go beyond that barrier. I sometimes sneaked up to the fence and called my sister. I would stay there for a long time, listening anxiously, but she never answered and I thought I could hear her cry inside. As time went on the secrecy surrounding my sister tightened and I sensed that something was awfully wrong with her. I could see it on the worried faces of my parents and gather it from the bustle that went on around her seclusion hut. My mother's older brother, a well-known witchdoctor, came and held weird rituals inside the compound. I could hear my sister's moaning and crying and went around with a scared feeling of helplessness.

"As usual when serious things happen in a family, the smaller children are pushed aside and nobody thinks of explaining to them what is going on. I had terrifying fantasies about what horrible things were being done to my beloved sister, and they were intensified beyond limits when finally she died and was buried without me being allowed to see her again. Much later my mother told me that my sister had suddenly taken ill while in confinement. She died before my parents were able to find effective help for her. To me the whole experience was a nightmare. I grieved for my sister and missed her. After that, being a *mwali* appeared to me a great mystery and a deadly ordeal and the thought that I would have to go through that myself filled me with horror. I thought out a thousand ways to conceal my maturation and fearfully waited for the first signs of the approaching puberty—it seemed like a death sentence to me.

"The tragic death of my sister was a severe shock to my parents and father decided to become a Christian. Since he had three wives, this meant great upheaval in the family as he could only keep one. During that time I was sent to live with my uncle, the same one who had treated my sister. You can imagine my fears about staying at his home. Remembering how my sister died, I anxiously tried to avoid him. I helped my aunt as best I could so that she would have nothing bad to tell him about me. With mounting anxiety I recognized that my puberty was drawing closer and during this time I visited a bush school not far from my uncle's place. There I heard for the first time of the mission boarding school where girls could stay throughout their puberty years. From then on I had only one desire: to be accepted into that school. I studied for my life, it seemed, and made sure the teacher noticed my eagerness. On the last school day I told the teacher my wish and asked him whether he could recommend me to the mission school. He liked the idea and promised to speak to my uncle. But my uncle would have nothing of it. Susanna is a girl, she

130

does not need more education, was his verdict. I felt desperate; time was running out and I was convinced I would die of fear if I was put in confinement.

"I knew there was no way I could persuade my uncle and so I sneaked away one day and ran home to my parents. Fortunately my father had retained my mother as his wife and she was eager to help me. To my great relief both my parents agreed to accompany me to the mission and upon my urging we set out the next day. My parents, of course, thought I had my uncle's consent as I did not tell them I had run away. I was accepted at the school and begged the nuns to let me stay there right away. They all laughed at my eagerness, not knowing how much it mattered to me to be a student before my parents found out that my uncle had already refused to let me go. I was so relieved to be within the protective walls of the mission school I did not even think about the family trouble I had stirred up. My uncle was furious when he learned that my parents had taken me to the mission without even consulting him. Being my mother's oldest brother he had, according to Wapogoro custom, the right to decide about me. A bitter feud started between the two families and has been going on ever since. To get me out of the school my uncle began to make arrangements for my marriage, but I stubbornly refused to consider any of the candidates he suggested. As I did not fear puberty any more I lived a happy carefree life with the other girls at the school. We loved our teachers and were eager to learn whatever they had to teach us. My only concern was that school would last only a few years. How should I face my uncle once I graduated? I did not realize the hardships my parents went through because of my refusal to marry. My uncle continued to insist on me marrying as it was his customary right to receive the bridal price. But my parents stood by me. They said that custom does not force a girl to marry against her wishes.

"During the time of these quarrels, a child of one of my sisters fell ill with epilepsy and everybody was convinced that my uncle had used witchcraft to avenge himself. My old fears were rekindled when I heard the news and I desperately looked for a way to escape his influence. I had become a Christian during my first year at the mission school and one day one of the nuns suggested that I should myself become a teacher and go to teacher's training college. How I relished that idea! Then I would not have to go home; I might be able to find work at the school I had come to like so much. I visited my parents and explained in glowing terms how much I wished to be a teacher. Again they promised to help me. But what could I do to pacify my uncle? He was actually the one who should help me with my tuition fees, but of course he was going to be angry again and deny me any assistance. I decided not to ask him for any money but to get it together myself. I had to work to earn money besides studying and sometimes I did not even have enough to eat. But my uncle would not leave me alone. He wrote ugly letters to me at the college and demanded the money I had denied him as the benefit of my bridal price. I was so afraid of the man, I scraped together every cent I could spare and sent him a few shillings. My parents suffered more than they would let me know under the hostility of my uncle and his relatives who would also have profited from the bridal money had I not refused to marry.

"When I graduated from college about a year ago I was immediately offered a position as teacher here. I returned in triumph to live with my parents, thinking that my uncle would respect me now. But he continued to harass me and threatened witchcraft when I refused to pay him any more. Then my father decided to take back one of his former wives and both my mother and I were indignant. Was he not a Christian? He knew that the Church allowed him only one wife. But my father knew that his former wife lived a miserable life after he had abandoned her, and his conscience was divided. I was very angry with him and my presence at home only increased the tension between my parents. I therefore decided to leave and to again live at the school. My parents did not say much, but they were both very unhappy when I left.

"Since I came back to live at the school my uncle has

132

again demanded money from me and threatened me with witchcraft if I do not obey his demands. Because I refused to give in, my father has already been struck by a terrible illness. He is still very sick and cannot walk any more. I feel terribly guilty towards my ailing father. I should never have blamed him for wanting his other wife back; he never blamed me for my actions. And now I have caused him this illness too. I know it is my uncle who bewitches my father to get back at me. It is my fault that my father has to suffer and now it is my turn." Susanna cried and wrung her hands in despair. I tried to think of a way to help her. What if she would take me to her father, I suggested. Maybe I could cure him. Susanna looked at me with hope in her eyes. But then she shook her head. "Your medicine won't help against *uchavi,*" she said with a disheartened expression on her face. I would not give in and persisted until she agreed to take me to her parents so I could at least examine her father.

Now that Susanna had poured out her heart and shared her troubles with me, she felt relieved and was not as anxious any more and a few days later we went to visit her parents in their village. It was very moving to observe the happiness of the old couple when seeing their daughter again. Unfortunately it turned out that the poor man had suffered a stroke. One side of his body was paralyzed and he had great difficulty talking. There was indeed not much modern medicine could do to help, but I did not have the heart to tell Susanna. Strokes are rarely encountered among these people and I felt that this man must have gone through unusually severe mental and emotional stress. First the loss of a daughter during her *mwali* period; perhaps he had felt guilty over her untimely death. Then the emotional upset of having to send away two of his faithful wives when he became a Christian. And during all these years having to endure the anger of his wife's relatives because he protected his emancipated daughter Susanna and let her have her own way. Finally to endure the disapproval of both his wife and daughter because he had felt compelled to help one of his former wives. In a way it was true that Susanna was at least partly responsible for her father's predicament and I felt it was essential for her to be actively involved in the care of her father. I discussed at length with her how she could help him to recover, prescribing different kinds of strengthening medicines and showing her how to do physiotherapy. She was very eager and at once decided to move back home so that she could spend all her spare time with him.

The old man was visibly pleased to have his daughter home again. He very quickly regained his spirits and in time recovered amazingly well. Susanna also appeared happier. One day she came to see me again and seemed more self-assertive than before. She appeared to have matured during these last weeks. Smilingly and with pride she told me how she had finally succeeded in appeasing her uncle. She had gone to his place and found him sitting outside his hut. Mustering all her courage, she had walked up to him and asked him what was the amount of money he had expected a suitor to pay as her bridal price. It was a considerable sum of money. In front of his family who had assembled to hear their discussion, Susanna produced the money and placed it in front of her uncle with the words, "Here is the money. With this I pay you my own bridal price. From now on you have no rights over me and it is up to me whether I am going to marry or not." The uncle was taken by surprise, but he accepted the money and agreed to settle the conflict between his family and her's. Every relative entitled to it was given his proper share of the bridal money.

The news that Susanna, the teacher, had purchased her freedom by paying her own bridal price spread among the people. They discussed this event for a long time and could not stop musing upon the following puzzle: the man who would want to marry Susanna—to whom was he going to pay the price for his bride?

15
Simon the Wazimu

About half an hour's drive into the mountains from Kwiro was the junior priest seminary Kasita, a boarding school with a curriculum much like that of an ordinary high school but more difficult as Latin and other subjects related to Christian theology were added so that the boys could transfer directly from there to the senior seminary near the capital. The seminary was situated away from the villages at the end of a lonely road winding through heavy forest. Its large white buildings stood alone on a mountain plateau, surrounded by lush gardens, fields and sports grounds, with the forest closing off the view again at the far end of the cultivated land. Fields and gardens were worked by the monks living there and the boys had to help them when not attending classes.

The teachers were priests and imposed strict discipline. Many boys, especially those who had enrolled for the sake of education rather than for the purpose of becoming priests, did not make it and dropped out after a few years. The contrast between the emotionally restricted atmosphere of the seminary and the lenient upbringing at home, where every female relative was a warm accepting mother to them, was more than

135

they could tolerate. Most of them entered the seminary at the age of ten or eleven after four or five years of primary school and they felt lost and frightened in the big rooms and empty halls of the seminary; no touch of a mother's hand had put any warmth or familiarity into it. The boys slept in large dormitories and a narrow bed and small wooden box with a few personal belongings was the only private space they had. They had little contact with their distant families since most of the boys were too far away from home to receive regular visits or to return there during the holidays. Boys whose families could not afford the necessary school fees had to remain at the school during their holidays and earn their fees by working around the seminary.

Early every morning students attended Mass and on Sundays there were several church services; the days were filled with work in class, in the study rooms or out in the gardens. Monks and teachers watched them everywhere; there was little room for jokes and laughter and their only recreation was music and sports. The seminarists formed beautiful choirs, and on the sports field they became happy, outgoing soccer and basketball players. I used to stop at the sports field to watch them play when I went to the seminary for my monthly medical visit and I always marveled that I found so few toe injuries when I saw the boys running around without shoes and kicking the hard ball with their bare feet. What I mostly had to treat the boys for were sore throats, colds, minor injuries and stomach troubles. Many complained of poor vision because eye glasses were a symbol of wisdom to these boys, and those who finally got a pair were envied by the others. I had to be one step ahead of the cunning boys to be able to pick out those who were only pretending and those who really needed glasses. I learned to test one at a time and to use different kinds of tests, so that they would not know exactly what to expect. It became a sort of a game and quite likely they did outsmart me sometimes. I am sure they discussed it in their dormitories and had many a good laugh about it.

I felt sorry for these boys who so desperately lacked the

136

warmth and security of their mothers. They had to cope with homesickness and with the resentment they were bound to feel, being young boys who had to live under so many rules and restrictions. When they awaited their turn in the waiting room they would quarrel, laugh and joke like other children, but as soon as a priest entered, they turned into subdued, respectful little pupils. I sensed the tension created in the boys by having to buckle down under authority, and I was thoroughly aware of how they enjoyed being cared for by me. Even the older and shyer adolescents would prolong their visits as long as they dared without risking teasing from the other boys.

I sometimes received very secret letters from boys in the seminary, written in awkward English:

Dear of mine! I am very glad to write this letter to you since you haven't written a letter to me. The purpose of writing this letter is to tell you that if I pass my examinations I shall tell you. I wonder what sort of a life you think I have in here without your presence. The very fact that I am doubtful whether you really care for me or not seems to me a sign that you are. ... I pray for you and for your family every day. You must not think me horrid for writing this letter to you. I am not thinking about myself nearly so much as about you. Dear mother, I am sure you will agree with me and it would be wiser for me to write letters to each other. I wish we could see each other every day. By doing this we would be doing right all around. Let me hear from you at once, great doctor and my mother at the same time. Please think of me all the time— your most loving son Simon, a boy born of woman for difficulties.

That letter touched me more than many similar ones I received, as I knew very well who Simon was. Everybody in the seminary knew Simon. He was a lively child emanating warmth and charm wherever he went. When Simon entered a room there would soon be smiles and laughter. He chatted as unaffectedly with Father Superior as with the youngest boy.

He knew he was the teacher's favorite, but bright as he was, he knew how to make himself well liked by the boys too, cracking jokes and making witty remarks. His sparkling personality seemed to stimulate the other boys. I had often found him rather trying, however, with his amazing energy and endless chatter.

Simon must have been about fifteen years old, but he was small of stature and in spite of his captivating charm, seemed immature and childish in many ways. The tone of his letter contrasted sharply with the detached gaiety he usually displayed and I was concerned about it, so I asked about Simon when I visited Father Superior in his library one day after work. I learned that the boy was from a small village some three days journey away and that he had entered the seminary at the age of ten. When he was a small boy he used eagerly to attend Mass at the little mission close to his home. The local priest noticed that the boy appeared to be deeply stirred by the divine service and made him an acolyte. Simon quickly learned the required Latin words and was so serious about his functions in the church that the Father suggested to the parents they send him to the seminary. An intense family quarrel ensued. Simon's grandfather who was a famous medicine man did not want the boy to become a priest. He had already chosen this grandson to be his successor. But Simon was afraid of his grandfather's incantations and looked up to the priest as his ideal. He defied his grandfather's wish and one day he left the village and turned up at the seminary asking to be admitted. Reluctantly the parents consented and Simon quickly became the teacher's favorite. He was convinced that the boy was predestined for priesthood.

Soon after Father Superior had told me about the boy he voiced some concern regarding his behavior. Simon seemed to have great difficulties falling asleep at night and would keep the other boys awake with his restless activities, pranks and long tirades. He spent hours in the Chapel, praying with a fervor that even the pious monks found exaggerated. In the classroom he could no longer sit quietly but constantly disrupted instruction with laughing and crying spells. I was convinced that Simon suffered from severe anxiety. Striving to be a good student, he strained himself to the utmost. Maybe homesickness, the stress of discipline and study and the prospect of priesthood was too much for this immature boy. I feared that he would have a mental breakdown and suggested to the Fathers that it might be best to send the boy home for a while. They hesitated, knowing of the discord in the family and that the boy did not want to leave. I ordered some light sedative for Simon and advised the Father to ease the pressure on the boy.

About a week later Simon was brought to my clinic from the seminary. He had shown increasingly erratic behavior and when he finally began shouting incomprehensible sentences, the teachers realized that the boy had indeed become mentally ill. The travel from the seminary to the mission upset the poor boy to such a degree that he lost all his wits. A stream of senseless words flowed from his lips and he ran aimlessly around in the dispensary gesticulating, screaming and laughing and scaring the other patients who fled outside and gathered in a curious crowd. I tried to catch Simon to calm him down. Suddenly he stopped in front of me and cried out, "Am I mentally ill?" and then more quietly, "Please Madam, give me some medicine." The nurse and I used the opportunity to give him a tranquilizing injection and when he became drowsy we led him to a small storehouse where we had a room for emergency patients. People followed us across the road, and soon a big crowd had formed. When Simon looked up and noticed the people, his agitation arose again and he yelled to them to go away, he wanted to be left alone. But they just stared at him in fascination and no words of persuasion made them disperse. As we were just about to enter the house, Simon jerked himself free with surprising strength. He threw himself to the ground, smeared his face with earth and mud and lapped up some dirty rainwater just like an animal. Then he prostrated himself and spoke with subdued, quivering voice, "Please, *Mama Mganga,* make me well again, will you?" His actions made the spectators freeze, horror on their faces. Nobody dared to move. I quickly raised the boy to his feet and we led him into the room. It took a while until Simon calmed down enough for us to put him to bed. Simon's older brother, who worked at the mission, came in and offered to look after him. Simon was glad to see him and gradually went to sleep with his brother sitting by his bedside. The people were still standing in groups outside when we finally left the two brothers. They looked at us in silence. A woman came up to me and whispered, "Be careful, *Mama Mganga,* that boy is turning into an animal." I looked into her anxious face and did not know what to answer. I shook my head and hurried back to the dispensary.

The next day Simon awoke in the early morning even more agitated than before. Fragments of sentences and words in English, Latin and Swahili poured from his lips in a confused babble. He tried to shut up by pressing both hands against his mouth to close it, but to no avail. He knelt down beside the bed and tried to pray, then suddenly he threw the pillow across the room at his brother, ripped the blankets off the bed and flung things around with incredible speed. Unable to restrain himself he held his hands to us and begged us to bind them. He was relieved when we finally tied him securely to his bed. But even after I had given him the highest tranquilizer dose I dared to use, he threw his head from one side to the other and continued to talk until foam appeared at his mouth. His brother attended to him gently, trying in vain to make him eat. People continued to arrive and obstinately squatted outside the house waiting to see what would happen. Towards evening Simon was exhausted, his voice had faded into a whisper, his lips were dry and cracked and he finally accepted some water from his brother. When I visited them late at night I thought that the medicine was taking effect.

Early in the morning, Simon's brother, hollow-eyed and strained from a long wake, came to me trembling with fear. He did not dare to stay any longer, he would have to take Simon home. What had happened? "Please come and see for yourself." I hurried over to the storehouse. Simon was crouching on his bed, arms and legs tucked under his body. He had a strange and tense expression on his face and his piercing eyes followed our slightest movements. When we slowly approached, he growled, indeed like an animal. People jostled at the door. We looked at each other. What could we do? Simon was getting increasingly agitated; it obviously bothered him to see people peering at him through the doorway. Suddenly he leaped to the floor on all fours letting out an incredible cry. It sounded like the roar of a lion. His voice was amazingly forceful. People dispersed with shrieks of terror. I seized the fragile boy and held him down, yelling at his brother to help me. We had to pin down his head, face to the floor, because he bared his teeth and tried to bite us. We succeeded in holding him until the nurse got him tied up again and then with great care we picked him up and put him to bed. He threw his head around, pounded the bed with fists and feet, growling and spitting, unable to recognize anybody around. Another injection brought an end to his terrible yells.

I tried to persuade the brother to let Simon stay. I was confident that in a few days the medicine would help to get the boy out of his manic state. But the brother looked anxiously at Simon and shook his head. We had both heard the lion's roar, he said. It was a spirit from the past who spoke through Simon. Someone in the family, maybe not even Simon himself, must have gravely offended an ancestral spirit. It was now a family affair that could not be solved far away from home. Simon would not get well before his grandfather, the medicine man, had seen him, consulted his healing spirits and corrected the offence against the ancestor so he could give Simon the right medicine. He, Simon's brother, could not take upon himself the responsibility of keeping Simon at the mission. Should the boy die, the family would never forgive him for not having brought Simon home in time. After much discussion, and as Simon was unable to express his wishes, I had to give in to the brother. With a heavy heart I prepared some medicine and food for the journey. The two boys had a long march ahead of them. How would Simon survive? The brother decided to use a shortcut through the mountains, so they might reach home in three days. As they stood there ready to leave I again asked the brother to consider letting Simon stay, but he declined, already impatient and anxious as he looked ahead to the difficult journey. Where would they sleep at night? Somewhere in the bush! Was he not afraid of the wild animals? The brother looked at me pensively. "The wild animals will not hurt us this time," he said in a soft voice, and then abruptly turned away as if he wanted to avoid further questions. I looked at the two brothers as they marched off, the older brother in front, in one hand the bundle with their provisions, the other firmly holding the rope to which Simon was tied. The latter followed with his hands tied together, singing and chatting as he staggered along pulled by the rope. I saw them turn off the road, making for the forest and the mountain slope. I certainly did not feel too good letting them go, but the people who had stayed around all this time had supported the brother and urged me to give in.

A few days after their departure we heard through the "bush telegraph" that the boys had reached their home more dead than alive. Simon had fought his brother several times and had scared people away from the villages they passed. The old grandfather had at once begun his divinations to find the cause of Simon's madness. A few weeks later a messenger came to Father Superior at the seminary to tell him that Simon had recovered completely from his illness. He would not return to the seminary as he had decided against priesthood. He had now become an obedient disciple of his grandfather, the medicine man, and would follow in the footsteps of this famous healer who had cured his madness.

As time went by I often wondered what Simon's brother had meant by his remark that the wild animals would not hurt them. I came to understand this much later through another dramatic event not directly related to the two brothers. It started out with rumors of a lion who had become very dangerous to people. Lions are respected and people know how to keep out of their way. These animals are usually not a great menace to human beings, preferring deer and other animals as their prey. But occasionally a lonely lion, who is too decrepit to hunt the swift animals, will attack man. We could often hear the lions roar at night down on the Ulanga plains, but it was very rare that lions made the mountain slopes their hunting grounds. Mountains are the domain of the leopards. But now there was a lion who had waited at a lonely path and killed a woman returning from the water hole. Apparently the lion had not been frightened by people shouting and throwing stones to chase him away. His behavior had been strange, people told us when coming to the dispensary. There is nothing people fear as much as an animal behaving in an unusual manner. They immediately suspect it of having supernatural powers. On Sunday after Mass village elders asked the Fathers to hunt and kill this lion, as they themselves did not dare to touch a supernatural animal. The lion disappeared, however, and people began to relax until suddenly he struck again.

This time he jumped from the dark into a courtyard where a family was sitting around the fire. Before the stunned people could move, he seized an old woman and disappeared with her. The terrified relatives could hear her screams as she was dragged along, until the poor woman met her fate in the lion's claws. Now people became hysterical. They flocked to the mission for protection, begging the Fathers to do something. Finally some of the best hunters went out searching for the beast, but it slyly avoided them, withdrawing somewhere far into the impassable mountain region, waiting for the excitement to die down. From then on people ventured out only in groups, and accompanied by young men carrying all kinds of weapons: spears, bow and arrows, axes, old rifles. Fear spread to all villages and people called upon their diviners to perform rituals to protect them from the supernatural lion. A feeling of caution gripped us all and we avoided long excursions away from the security of the mission. When I had to visit sick people in a village, I made sure to be back before dark and to let the mission know where I went in case I would be late. Generally however, I did not give the lion much thought and was amused at the men with their knives and rifles who surrounded me wherever I visited and bravely assured me I had nothing to fear; they would protect me from the lion.

Then suddenly one day it was no fun any more! I was examining a patient in a hut when I suddenly heard a mighty roar outside. For some reason this time the lion did not charge right away and people had time to run away. Fortunately I was already indoors for I could hardly have reacted as quickly as the villagers did. They literally dived headlong into the hut and in a moment the room was full of panting people. Breathless and with pounding hearts we heard the lion roar in disappointment and then sniff around the huts as he went along. In the tense quietness that followed we suddenly heard a voice. It was unmistakably the voice of a man singing as he came closer. He was obviously unaware of the lion waiting for prey somewhere behind a hut. Maybe the man was a villager returning home, I thought. I looked at the people around; their faces were ash grey and their eyes were bulging with fear. Nobody moved, nobody said a word. The singing became louder—the man was coming closer. I made a move. Someone had to warn him. An old man grasped my arm. "Stay, *Mama Mganga,*" he whispered, "the lion will not harm that one." It struck me that I had heard something like that before. I listened intently. The song sounded very silly. The man seemed to babble non-sensical words and we could hear him laughing and talking to himself in between his singing. He was unmistakably insane! I could hardly restrain myself from rushing outside to warn him, but the old man, sensing my intention, held me firmly and shook his head. I felt sick to my stomach. Unable to make a decision I expected to hear the dreadful thump and a cry as the lion jumped at the man. But it did not happen. For a long while we heard the madman's voice and his shuffling feet. He called for someone, probably astonished to find nobody around. Finally his voice faded away somewhere at the other end of the village. The lion had indeed let him pass without

144

doing him any harm.

Night was falling and made us even more frightened. For a long, long time everybody remained quiet and waited, but at long last somebody moved, at first very carefully. As nothing happened, people became a bit braver, and finally a fire was lit and spread light and warmth around. We all relaxed. Amazing how reassuring the flames of a living fire can be! The lion did not appear as terrifying any more. People regained their courage; the lion would not attack a house which smelled of smoke, they told each other. Women put their kettles on the fire and since I had to stay until the men from the mission came for me, they invited me to share their meal. When everyone had eaten and the fire was bright and warm I turned to the old man and asked him how he had known that the lion would not harm the singing man. Silence fell, everybody looked at the old man and he thought about the question for a while. When he began to talk, he spoke slowly as if he had to think over carefully each word he was going to say. I listened attentively, knowing that these people found it extremely unpleasant to explain something and then to find out that it was not understood. It often seemed to me as if they thought of words as living beings which should not be wasted. If words are used carelessly and not heard, they drop to the floor and are lost. That should not happen, especially with important words.

"We have a word for our ancestral spirit, *mzimu,*" the old man slowly began. "Now *wazimu* means being possessed by a spirit. But *wazimu* is also the word for a mad man. Do you see? To us, a person who acts insane is possessed by a forceful spirit. Mostly this spirit belongs to one of our ancestors who is angry because of some insult we have caused him. Our diviner has to find out what we did wrong. Sometimes he cannot find the cause, and then the person will not be cured. We also know that an ancestral spirit can go into an animal. This lion which has supernatural power might well be possessed by an ancestral spirit seeking revenge. When meeting each other, the insane and the lion recognize and respect each other. Being of the same nature they have a special communication. Sometimes a mad man can change into an animal. We fear and respect both of them, but we do not want them around. They are a menace to all of us. How do we know it was not the lion who went around singing and laughing out there? We feel helpless against both. We want to get rid of them, to kill them, but we do not know whether it would help. The spirit might just punish us some other way." The old man fell silent. There was an anxious, tense atmosphere in the room. People drew closer together around the fire. These were dangerous things to talk about, things one should not mention to strangers. I felt that the people had shown a good deal of confidence in me by letting the old man talk like this. I broke the silence by telling them about Simon and what had happened to him. When I mentioned how the brother of Simon had assured me that no wild animal would hurt them even when they had to sleep unprotected in the forest, they all nodded, and I thanked the old man for having explained things to me.

The quietness which now followed was friendly. I think we all felt that we trusted each other and shared in something important. "Respect for the ancestors and knowledge of tradition and of what is right and what is wrong is necessary to be able to live a life tolerably free of fear." The old man seemed to speak more to his own people than to me. "The ancestor's spirit can take revenge upon anyone in the family. This is to remind us that we must share responsibility for each other's actions and that we have to keep together if we want to survive. We have to always remember what is right and what we have inherited from our ancestors. If our young people try to break away and are unwilling to obey our elders, they have to pay the price, even if that is to become insane." We were so absorbed in listening to what the old man said, that we did not hear the noise outside and were startled when the men from the mission appeared in the doorway. With rifles and torches they had come to accompany me home. I think we all regretted the interruption. The terrifying experience we had been through together, the meal we had shared around the fire and the secret things we had discussed made us feel very close to each other. Everybody followed me on the way and shook my hand when we parted at the end of the village.

The hunters renewed their efforts, and a few days later they came upon the lion and killed him with a few shots. To make sure the people believed the lion was killed, he was laid out in the yard of the police station, the body spread out and the mighty head resting on a stone. He was a formidable animal. People filed past him and stood around in small groups admiring the dead lion and whispering respectfully to each other. They seemed to regret that the majestic animal had been killed, and they paid homage both to the animal and to the spirit they thought had dwelt in it.

16
The Invincible Diviner

A few years before I arrived at the Kwiro mission a small outpost had been established among the plains tribe of the Wangindo in a very remote area. The Father in charge of this station came to the mission where I worked about once a month for fresh supplies and often invited me to visit his outpost at Luhombero, not only because he needed my help, but because he thought I would find it interesting to work among these people. The tribe had practically had no contact with the outside world until the arrival of the Father and a friar who began to build kilns and to produce bricks for house construction. The local people showed great interest and many young men came to help them and to learn the trade. Some erected their own houses with the new material. But apart from a few families, not many of the tribesmen were eager to convert. They were still hunters and their villages were spread out over a large area. The people were neither Christians nor Islamic but adhered to their own traditional beliefs. However, many sent their children to the mission school, saying: "Let our children be taught new ways; let them become Christians if they want to, but we oldtimers prefer to remain the way we are."

148

All tribesmen were grateful for the medical help offered by the mission since there were no other treatment facilities that far away from modern civilization. Whether the Father liked it or not, he had become deeply involved in treating the sick, assisted only by a dresser at the small mission dispensary. They were both pleased to present to me their most difficult cases, and the Father took me along on his regular safaris by motorbike to distant villages. People very much appreciated our visits and when they heard the *picki-picki,* as they called the motor bike, they would assemble in the village square with their sick. Sometimes they asked me to come along to their huts if the patient happened to be too ill to be moved. Most of the people spoke only their tribal language, but there were always one or two children in the village who knew some Swahili, and who had to be the go-betweens. Our mutual struggle to understand each other gave rise to much goodnatured laughter and people thanked us with small presents. Mostly they brought rice, eggs, chicken and other foods, but at times they also gave me artifacts like a drum, a carved walking stick or a homemade basket. The amount of supplies one could take along on such field trips was, however, quite limited. Sometimes we ran out of gas with our small motor bike and we then had to walk for miles in the sun. We therefore encouraged the people to bring their sick ones to us at the mission.

It was amazing how the people changed when they came to the mission. At home in their villages they were relaxed, friendly and quick to laugh, but when arriving at the mission they lost their self-confidence and became fearful and apprehensive. Everything about the mission seemed to scare them and it was always a struggle to have them stay long enough for proper treatment. Numerous taboos and proscriptions complicated living arrangements when families from different villages had to stay together in one place. I tried to understand the motivation behind their behavior but usually they would only answer: "The *mbui* says we have to do it this way." The *mbui,* diviner, seemed to have great influence over his people and the dresser informed me that sick people always consulted him before they would come to the dispensary. Each time there was some small misunderstanding between us, anxiety flared up and we seemed to be dealing with unexpected crisis situations all the time.

One day a large group of people arrived from a far-off village bringing with them a sick girl. The men carried their bow and arrows, the women big loads of food and straw mats on their heads. The women kept at a distance hiding behind the men, mothers holding on to their children as if they were afraid I might touch them. Together with the people at the mission I mustered the newcomers as they assembled outside the dispensary. Just to have a look, I pulled out an arrow from the quiver a man carried in a sling around his shoulder. At that moment people dropped everything and ran for their lives, and in a few seconds not a soul could be seen. I stood baffled. What had happened? Everybody had disappeared. "Put down the arrow *Mama Mganga,* don't touch it, leave it on the ground and come here!" It was the urgent voice of the dresser from inside the dispensary where he too had taken refuge. I looked at the arrow. Its point was blackened, I noticed. I placed it on the ground and walked over to the dispensary. The yard remained deserted until the dresser went outside and called out that *Mama Mganga* did not intend to harm anybody. She did not know it was a poison arrow. Finally the man who owned the arrow came forth. He approached slowly and with caution, keeping his eyes fixed on the door of the dispensary, ready to flee again at the slightest movement there. Not before he had secured his arrow did he call the others to come out of hiding. They were unable to overcome their fear and distrust of me, however, and I very much regretted my thoughtless action. In vain we tried to persuade them to stay or to leave the sick girl with us. As soon as I had given her some medication they picked her up and hastened back to their village.

After work that day I asked the dresser to tell me more about the poison arrows and why the people had been so frightened. He explained to me that the poison on the arrow

150

was extremely potent. Even the slightest scratch inflicted by such an arrow would be deadly. The Wangindo hunters used it to kill their game. It did not matter where the arrow hit, a few seconds later the animal would shiver, collapse and die. As I later found out, the arrow poison contains the cardiotoxic substance *ouabain* which kills the prey without spoiling the meat. The poison is extracted from the sap of a tree, and only some trees at certain times of the year will yield enough of the poison to make it worthwhile. The trained hunter will spot such a tree on travels in the bush because he finds dead insects and birds lying under it. Keeping his find secret, the hunter extracts the sap and prepares a decoction, the recipe for which nobody outside the tribe knows. The hunter has a hazardous method of testing the strength of the poison. He makes a small cut below his knee and lets blood trickle down his leg. At the ankle he places a sample of the poison. As soon as the blood reaches the poison, a reaction takes place, discoloring the blood as the poison creeps upwards along the blood streak. The strength of the poison determines how quickly it will move upwards. Just before it reaches the wound, the man scrapes off poison and blood with one sweeping movement of his bush knife. Should he for some reason hesitate and not act fast enough so that the poison reaches the cut and gets into the bloodstream, he would be dead within seconds. Such accidents were known to have happened, the dresser told me. The poison is mixed with adhesive materials, smeared on the arrow heads and dried in the sun. The hunter takes along two or three such arrows on his hunting trips. They are placed in a special quiver and the man never parts from it as long as he is on the way. At home, or if he stays with friends, he keeps it securely hidden. No wonder the people had been terrified by my rash action!

One morning there was again a turmoil in the yard. I hurried out and found the Father in the middle of a large crowd. People were agitated and appeared outright hostile. For a moment I thought they were going to attack him, but when they saw me approach they made way and fell silent. I

151

could feel the tension building up. The Father turned to me, looking quite embarrassed. "People tell me that a newly buried body from the cemetery has been dug out and the grave has been desecrated. Although they do not dare to say so directly, people seem to think that you have something to do with it. Somebody saw you walking out there in the dark." I felt hot; it was true, I had been walking past the graveyard the night before. It had been such a beautiful moonlit night, I had taken a stroll in the cool evening not thinking anything about passing the cemetery behind the church. Since that incident with the poison arrow, people had been quite uneasy about me; they probably thought I was a witch using cadavers for some sinister purpose as sorcerers were expected to do.

The crowd grew and people appeared terribly upset. Anxiously I asked the Father whether it might be wiser for me to leave the area, when I suddenly noticed a change in the mood of the crowd. They had turned their attention to a newcomer who addressed them eagerly. We could not understand what he was saying, but the people calmed down and soon dispersed, many looking embarrassed and bewildered. We asked the cook, who was always well informed, what had been said. The man, he told us, had come with a message from the diviner. The *mbui* had announced that the grave was opened by hyenas. No person was to be blamed for the disappearance of the corpse, except perhaps for the men who dug the grave and failed to close it properly. Again it seemed to me that this diviner had great power over the people and I asked the dresser whether he thought there would be a chance for me to see this man. He was not sure, but promised he would let it be known that *Mama Mganga* wished to meet with the famous *mbui*.

Time passed, but there was no response. Then much later, on another visit to the area, I happened to treat one of the diviner's close relatives. We were just having our evening meal when the cook reported the arrival of an important family with a sick member. The patient was a very old man and it was easy to see that his days were numbered. I was rather surprised that he was brought to the mission since old people usually preferred to die at home. After having examined him I explained to the family that he was going to die, but the old man himself insisted on wanting to stay under my care. I agreed to keep him only if some of his relatives would stay and help look after him. After much talk two men stepped forward and presented themselves as the patient's brother and his son. We had them carry the old man to an empty storehouse where they could stay with him and we provided them with firewood so they could make a fire on the stone floor to keep the old man warm during the cool night. Later in the evening I went to see the patient. To my great surprise and indignation I found the brother and his son sitting outside beside a blazing fire, while the sick old man was lying in the dark, shivering in his wet rags on the cold cement floor of the storehouse. I could not help scolding the two men at the fire but they did not move to help me while I cleaned up the mess on the floor and brought a straw mat and a blanket for the patient. The old man thanked me and when he was a bit more comfortable he fell asleep.

As I continued to upbraid the men outside, they hung their heads and waited for me to calm down. The expression on their faces was genuinely sorrowful. Finally the patient's brother lifted his head and looked at me with sad eyes. *"Mama Mganga,"* he said in a mild voice, "this dying man is my oldest brother. Many years ago he infringed upon my rights with my wife and they had a son." He nodded at the youngster sitting motionless and staring into the fire. Then he continued. "When we started to make the fire and wanted to sit with him in the room my brother said, 'Brother, it is not wise of you to stay with me now. Remember the words of the *mbui* when we brought our troubles before him at the time I wronged you. You are the oldest, the *mbui* said to me, you'll die first. Because of your misdeed you will have to die alone, since anybody of your close family staying with you when you have to go would be accused of having used witchcraft. Therefore my brother, leave me alone now. You can sit with our son outside the hut, but let *Mama Mganga* take care of me.'" I was moved by the strange beauty of this family tragedy now drawing to its end. I understood why the old man had chosen to die away from his family; he wanted to avoid new quarrels breaking out because of suspicions surrounding his death.

Everyday I went down to the storehouse to see the old man. He was quickly going downhill, but I could at least make his last days a bit more comfortable. In the evening I used to sit for a while with his brother and son to wait for the patient to fall asleep. The two men were happy to have company during the lonely watch and they tried to keep me there as long as possible. When the old man finally died and the two returned home, the brother of the deceased man said to me, "I have heard you want to meet our *mbui*. He is my cousin. When we have returned home, I will let him know how kindly you treated us here and how you helped my brother in his last days. He may well grant you a visit." And indeed a few days later, the young boy returned and asked to speak to me alone. The *mbui,* he said, had agreed to see me if I could arrange the visit in such a way that nobody else would know of it. The boy was to take me there. We decided I should prepare as for one of my medical safaris, and we would set out early the next morning. That night I could hardly sleep. Since I could not tell anybody where I was going, not even the dresser or the Father, I would be completely at the mercy of my escort. But the taste for adventure overcame my doubts and we departed as if I was to visit a patient in a village.

We had to walk a long distance since the diviner's compound was in a secluded place in the foothills of the Sali Mountains. After we had passed the last village, the boy turned off the road and led me through a thick forest on a hardly visible path. Winding its way along the hillside it ended at a cluster of huts under huge mango trees. Before entering the compound the boy asked me to wait while he announced our arrival. My heart was pounding, not only from our brisk march, but from anticipation of what would follow. Now at the destination I could not help feeling apprehensive and I tried to think of what I was going to say when facing the *mbui*.

The boy returned with a ceremonial scarf placed over his shoulder and took me to a seat under the mango trees. I saw a frail figure draped in a red blanket coming out of the largest hut and approaching me slowly. This must be him, I thought, and wanted to stand up to greet him, but with an authoritative gesture he bid me to remain seated. He did not extend his hand as was customary, but sat down in the sun well outside the shadow of the trees. His hair was black and the skin of his face smooth like that of a youth, his searching eyes bright and clear. Only the depigmented dry skin of his legs betrayed his advanced age. He greeted me with dignity and sat quietly waiting for me to speak. Women and children gathered around him but kept at a respectful distance.

The reserved manner of the *mbui* and the inquisitive glances of the people surrounding him only heightened the tension I felt. It was difficult to gather my thoughts and put them in appropriate Swahili but I finally succeeded in expressing my thanks for having been granted this visit. I felt embarrassed about my language when he replied in perfect Swahili. He started out with formal phrases; he was glad I had come the long way to pay him a visit; he hoped the journey had not been too unpleasant or hot. Having answered thus, he was again silent, leaving the initiative to me. It was indeed very hot. Insects swarmed around and irritated me with their stings. Each time the slightest breeze moved the branches above me, ripe mango fruits came tumbling down. I could hear the hard fruits rattle through the leaves on their way down and waited nervously for some of them to fall on me. Judging from the loud thud when they hit the ground, I gathered it would be pretty painful to have one fall on my head. Later somebody told me that it was kind of a test the *mbui* let his visitors undergo by placing them under the mango trees. Those who sat stoically and unperturbed were deemed to have a strong spirit, especially if they were not hit by a falling fruit. Mine must have been fairly strong, since the mangos, smashing down and cracking open right and left of me, never hit me. After some time I did forget about them as I was trying hard to keep up the conversation.

I told the *mbui* that I was impressed by the wise counsel he had given to patients I saw. Could he explain what was the difference between a *mbui* like him and a *mganga,* medicine man? My words seemed to please him. He thought about my question for a while before he answered. "It is true that I too use herbs on certain occasions," he began, "but my task is to find the causes of illness rather than to cure them." He paused, but since I did not say anything he continued, "Sickness and death have many causes. If they are caused by the supreme spirit *mlungu,* then it is fate and nobody is to blame or can do anything about it. If ancestral spirits have been offended, I can divine and perform rituals according to our custom to help the victim find out what has been done wrong. At other times the affliction is caused by sorcery, *uchavi,* or by poison. I cannot cure witchcraft, but I can trace the culprit and advise the victim's family which *mganga* should be called, how to placate the sorcerer and what kinds of gifts and services are necessary to obtain the medicine which will cure the victim or take away the spell. Illness might be caused by the sick person himself. When he comes to me for help I will withdraw to my *ludewa* and ask my helping spirits for the wisdom to understand that person, his whole life situation and what went wrong." "What is the *ludewa?*" I asked as the *mbui* made a pause. He looked at me and hesitated. He turned to the boy who had accompanied me and said something to him at which the boy went into the *mbui's* hut and brought out a wooden box which he placed before him. Out of it the old diviner took a small bottle-gourd with a round hole in one end. He blew over the opening and the gourd gave a hollow sound. He listened attentively. "The tune is good, we can go," he said to the boy. Then he turned to me again, now with a more friendly expression. "You can come with me. I will show you my *ludewa.*"

A narrow path behind his hut took us into the forest again. Only the boys followed us as we climbed up the hill; the women and girls stayed behind. I had the hardest time to keep up with the light footed old man who walked ahead. I felt unbearably hot from climbing in the mid-day sun and just as I was close to giving up, exhausted, we came to an opening in the forest. A small well-built hut stood in the center of the place with wooden sticks arranged in a pattern around it. "This is a holy place," said the *mbui* in a solemn voice, "nobody can dwell here unharmed unless I take them along. This is my *ludewa*, where I meet my ancestral spirits. In the days of my grandfather many years ago, a warrior pursued by his enemies fled into this forest. They followed his tracks until suddenly his footsteps disappeared where the shrine is now standing. The spirits had taken him away and that was a sign that here was a meeting place for ancestral spirits of the warrior's tribe.

"My grandfather who was a famous *mbui* made this place his sanctuary. Every thing here, the trees and plants, the water in the stream and the very air itself has healing power. A person in trouble will undergo a purifying ceremony and sleep here at night. The spirits of his ancestors will appear to him in sleep. The next morning he tells me his dream and I help him understand the message conveyed to him. At other times I go to this sacred grove by myself to perform rites and to ask my ancestral spirit helpers why somebody is ill. They may advise me to prepare some medicine for the patient and his family to take. Or I might have everybody in the family, old and young, even the smallest baby come here to the sanctuary. Behind the *ludewa* is a little stream where I can dam the water so that it forms a pool. I will shave everybody's head and throw the hair into the pool. Then they all have to take a ritual bath in the clear water. Afterwards, while they watch me, I open the dam and let the water run out. As the water washes away the hair and dirt from their body, so their guilt and wrongdoings are swept away down the river. I try to re-establish peace between the people according to our custom. Whatever the dispute is about—a barren wife, an unfaithful spouse, a disrespectful child or even a land-claim—we have to abide by the rules inherited from our ancestors."

The *mbui* beckoned me to come inside his *ludewa*. I saw bundles of roots and dry branches in one corner and in another a group of gourds similar to the one he had used before to sound out the spirits. Dried leaves and fruits of a kind I did not know were suspended from the ceiling. There was an overpowering smell of herbs. I saw no firepit with ashes as in ordinary dwellings, only a few straw mats along the wall to sleep on. The *mbui* had in the meantime seated himself on the ground, the children standing behind him. I noticed that they all had spots which looked as if made of red clay, on their foreheads. When I joined them outside and the *mbui* smiled in a friendly way, I asked him what the marks were there for. He looked fondly at the children and explained, "Dreams have great significance and bad dreams may forebode unhappy events. My medicine against dreams which I apply to the children's foreheads protects them from accidents and illness. People come to tell me their dreams," the *mbui* continued. "Before going on a hunting trip or making an important decision, the head of a family will tell me his dreams, so that I can advise him what actions to take. Sometimes dreams warn the dreamer that he will be hit by an illness. Then I will ask my helping spirits whether somebody wants to harm the man and what could be done to avoid it. I might find out the culprit when an accident occurs but when the case is too complicated I have to use the water ordeal to discover the guilty person."

I looked at the old diviner. Should I dare ask further questions? He seemed relaxed and friendly and this was a chance I might never have again. "What is the water ordeal?" I asked.

"Well, let us say a man comes to me because he feels sick. The medicine man has not been able to help him. Maybe he has been at the mission to get some modern medicine, but he does not feel any better. Now he has had some nasty quarrels with his first wife for some time. He suspects her of wanting to harm him, perhaps by poisoning his food. He does not, however, dare to accuse her openly for fear of the consequences should she be innocent. After he has told me about his sus-

158

picions, I might decide to perform the water ordeal. I will announce that my ancestral spirits have told me that somebody is out to harm the man, and will summon all the villagers. Wood and water fixed in a special ceremony is brought to a crossroad outside the village where everybody has assembled. The wood is used to make a fire and boil the water in a big kettle, and when I have prepared myself, all the villagers file past the kettle. The sick man stands at my side and as each person walks past he will ask me, "Is this the wrongdoer?" and I will dip a twig in the boiling water and sprinkle it on my hand. If the person before me is free of guilt the water will not hurt me. But when the culprit is before us, the water drops suddenly burn my skin and I utter a cry. Then everybody knows who is the guilty one. If it should turn out to be the man's wife I will ask both of them to come to my *ludewa* for a special ceremony and I will do my best to reconcile them. I might warn the couple not to bring further misfortune on their family and remind them of the ancestors' wrath. I will prepare a special meal which they have to eat together as a sign that they will bury their grudges. People also come to me to learn how to appease angry spirits, because I am the one who knows the traditional ways. I received my knowledge from my grandfather and my father and will pass it on to young men who have the desire and the strength to become a *mbui*."

The old diviner looked at the boy adorned with the ceremonial scarf and smiled. "It's time to take *Mama Mganga* back," he said, "I am going to stay here for a while." He stretched out his hand and took mine. Turning the palm of my hand up he looked at it for a while. "You have much to learn yet," he muttered, then he looked me in the eye and said: "Remember to be fearless and patient." My face reddened and I felt my ears glowing. Could the old *mbui* have seen that I had too much fear and not enough patience? He smiled at me and there was kindness in his eyes. Before I was able to say something, he turned away and went into his *ludewa*.

I walked back with the boy in silence, overwhelmed and deeply impressed by what I had seen and heard. Not before we were close to the mission did I find words to express some of my thoughts. "How is it possible that your *mbui* could speak so openly to a stranger like me?" I asked the boy. "He knows that many missionaries and others do what they can to convert his people to Christianity or Islam, thereby turning the people away from their traditional beliefs and customs." "Yes, he knows," said the boy with a smile, "but he feels stronger than the missionaries." As I looked a bit doubtful, the boy went on to tell me that many years ago there was an old Father at the mountain mission who had become increasingly angry about the powerful *mbui* whom he thought to be a conservative force interfering with his missionary work. One day this Father decided to challenge the *mbui* face to face and to show him whose faith was stronger. He set out to look for the *mbui* in his sanctuary. To make sure he would find the way, he took along a few local people. But as they approached the *ludewa* the guides began to tremble and one after the other refused to accompany the Father any further. Finally they had all left, but the determined priest marched on by himself until he found the *mbui* already waiting for him at the *ludewa*. What was said between the two nobody knows, but the good Father got beside himself with rage and blindly tore down the sanctuary, throwing around the herbs and gourds and everything else he found in it. The *mbui* only sat quietly while the priest went berserk. It was in the middle of the day and very hot. The old Father was terribly upset. He became confused and when he wanted to return home, he could not find his way. Finally the *mbui* himself led the helpless priest safely back to the mission, with dignity and without reproaching him for what he had done. It was said that the Father never fully recovered from his crusade, while the *mbui* quietly rebuilt his shrine. People believe that it was the *mbui's* spirit helpers who avenged themselves upon the Father. After this event the *mbui* was even more respected among the people who from now on called him *mbui mshindi,* the invincible diviner.

160

17
In the Shadow of a Tree

Having lived for awhile in the fresh air of the Mahenge mountains, the hot, humid climate of the coast seemed unpleasant and exasperating to me, and I was reluctant to leave the mountain mission. But a priest at a small outpost south of Dar-es-Salaam sent a message to me that he had some very sick people and needed medical advice. I was to travel in one of the trucks commuting regularly between headquarters in town and the outpost mission. Happily, the driver turned out to be a Father I knew who planned to visit his friend the priest at the same small mission station near Kilwa.

It was during the rainy season and traveling on the unpaved coastal road would be tedious and even hazardous, so we decided to set out early in the morning, hoping to reach our destination before the hot afternoon sun made traveling an ordeal. During the night, however, it poured with rain and the next day we had to wait until the sun dried up the worst water puddles. Still the road was slippery and the heavily loaded truck skidded from one side of the road to the other. Going down steep hills I caught myself holding my breath and stiffening my muscles as if this would help to keep the truck on the road. On approaching the Rufiji River we found that it had overflowed its banks and flooded the fields. The water stood about one foot high on the road. The young boys who had been sitting on top of the loaded truck laughing and commenting on the Father's driving skills now slid down and waded in front of us to show him where to drive through the murky waters.

We reached the ferry landing without mishaps and looked for the ferry which was to take us across. There appeared to be some difficulties with a car on the other side, for we could see people standing on the riverbank gesticulating and running up and down. We had to swallow our impatience and prepare for a long wait, so we joined our good-humored boys in the shadow of a tree. As everywhere in the African bush, people turned up seemingly from nowhere and soon we were surrounded. They asked who we were and where we were going. As soon as they found out I was *Mama Mganga* some boys darted off towards a distant village, water splashing high as they ran. After a while a little procession came slowly marching towards us from the direction of the village. As they drew closer I could distinguish two men carrying a crudely made stretcher, presumably with a sick person. A burden descended upon my shoulders as I nervously watched them approach; who knew what problem they were bringing to me! The men put the stretcher down in front of me and the women and children who had come along stood around. The sick person was completely covered by a blanket in protection from the sun, and as I pulled it aside I was gripped with fear. Sleeping sickness! I knew it right away; the man held his arms and legs flexed in the typical posture of a patient in the terminal stage of the disease.

Sleeping sickness is caused by the parasite *trypanosoma gambiense* and is transmitted to humans from the blood of wild animals through the tse-tse fly, *glossina morsitans*. The painful bite of this fly is the nightmare of anybody traveling in *trypanosoma* infested regions. The parasite, once in the bloodstream, will infiltrate vital organs, producing toxic in-

162

flammation in the heart, the bone marrow and the spleen, causing excruciating pain and weakness. It has a special affinity to brain tissue and once having taken a hold there causes the typical stuporous sleep which gives the disease its name. The emaciated man before me was in this last phase of the dreaded illness. He was asleep and when I tried to awaken him he uttered a few confused words with a slurred voice but did not wake up completely. Clumsily he tried to ward off my touch with trembling hands. His swollen face had a stupefied expression. I knew it was too late; there was nothing I could do. Had he been brought to a hospital sooner he might have had a chance. The specific medication, a drug containing arsenic, can only be tolerated by patients in good general condition; it would kill this man now.

It is painful to have to admit to oneself that there is no hope for a patient and I knew from experience that these people would never accept such a verdict. They would believe that I did not want to treat the patient for some reason. Their friendliness would quickly turn into hostility and the news of my unwillingness to help one of them would travel fast and reach the mission station long before my arrival, making it nearly impossible for me to treat patients there. All this went through my mind as I stood there in the shadow of the tree, looking at the poor man. I knew he would go on sleeping until his death which was probably only a few days ahead. I quickly made up my mind to give this man an injection of a vitamin B preparation; it would do some good to his emaciated body. "This man is very ill;" I turned to the older men who had brought the patient. "I will have to give him a *dawa ya sindano.*" I could see approval on their faces. *Sindano* is the Swahili word for needle, and *dawa ya sindano* means medicine given by injection. To the people's understanding, only the most powerful medicines are given this way. Sick people would often ask me for a *sindano* without being the least concerned about what they were given.

The family looked on in deep silence as I performed the usual "ritual" of preparation. They stood motionless as I spread out a clean cloth on the ground, unwrapped the box with medicines, took the syringe from its alcohol filled container, mounted a needle, filed off the point of the vial and then drew up the liquid medicine. Eager and gentle hands turned the patient on his side. As I cleaned the skin with alcohol and slowly injected the liquid into the muscles, I looked at the men helping me. I thought I could read in their sad eyes that they knew the sick man was going to die. Surely they must have felt that I knew it too. It was as if we had a gentleman's agreement to say nothing but to give the dying man the *sindano* for the sake of his family. At least the distressed relatives would have the soothing feeling that everything possible had been done for him.

While the others prepared for the return to the village I spoke to the two older men. I warned them to look out for early symptoms of sleeping sickness in other villagers. I told them to pay attention to people complaining of headaches, fever, general weakness and pain in the heart and in the bones. If a person with such symptoms developed fast heartbeat and swollen glands, he should be suspected of having contracted sleeping sickness and should be taken to a hospital. I assured the anxious men that medical treatment could be quite successful if the disease was treated in its early stage. The men listened attentively and before leaving grasped my hand with both of theirs, thanking me profoundly with tears in their eyes. I could see the little group of people wading homewards through the flooded fields as we were slowly ferried across the river.

The Father told me that the forest and savannah around here were full of big game. They made up a vast reservoir for the protozoa causing sleeping sickness. The government health services had urged people to clear the bush for an area a mile wide around the villages to keep the tse-tse flies away from the huts, but the men who went out hunting could not avoid being bitten. In areas where the game was massively infested about one third of the flies would carry the deadly *trypanosoma*. Still, only some people bitten by such carriers

164

will actually develop the fatal type of sleeping sickness we had just seen. Others may only suffer from a slight malaise. Their lymph glands will successfully conquer the invader before it has a chance to spread to other organs.

Badly shaken by what we had witnessed, the Father was speeding up to get through this inhospitable region. Being less cautious, he overlooked a shallow spot on the road where the sun had not yet dried the surface. The truck skidded helplessly and before the driver could prevent it, one of the front wheels sank deep into the slough and we were stuck. We all had to get off. I stood in the scorching sun and watched the sweating boys unload the truck and pile the goods at the roadside. Not before the truck was completely empty did they succeed in jacking it up and lifting the wheels out of the mud. They had to chop off branches and place them in front of the wheels to prevent the truck from sliding into the mud again as the Father carefully maneuvered it onto safe ground. While we waited myriads of mosquitos feasted on our arms and legs. I did not mind them too much though. I knew that I was immune to their stings as I never missed taking the antimalaria medicine. It was the tse-tse fly which made me nervous. Anxiously I watched for the brownish insects. They had the habit of sitting in wait on smooth, sunwarmed surfaces from which point they suddenly dive for their victim, aiming at the nape of the neck or some other place difficult to reach. Their bites cause intense pain and a shiver of fear down the spine. The driver of a car is especially vulnerable as he can not watch out for the insects or take his hands off the steering wheel quickly enough to chase the vigilant flies away. In spite of our watchfulness we had all received a few agonizing bites when we finally were ready to drive on. Our fear made us keep the truck windows tightly shut as we drove through the tse-tse infested bush, even though we were nearly cooking in the overheated cabin.

It was already afternoon and the sun was shining merci-lessly at us through the front window. My head was burning and I felt nauseated; my skin became flushed and oversensi-tive from heat, moisture and the many mosquito stings. The

165

ghastly sight of the man dying from sleeping sickness would not leave me and made me sick at heart. I could not help wondering if by now one of us might be harboring those deadly parasites. Of course the chances were small, but the Father must have had the same thoughts because he asked me what would be the earliest signs of an infection. To boost our spirits I told him about the newly developed medicine *pentamidine* which, if given early, cures the type of sleeping sickness we had seen. At any rate the incubation period was twenty-one days, I explained, and we would by then be back in town and could have a blood test if we noticed a swelling around the site of the fly bite or a slight rash on the skin, symptoms indicating that the fly had been carrying *trypanosoma*.

The Father fell silent and I did not know whether he felt as miserable as I did, but when we passed through a village and I asked him to stop for a moment to breathe some fresh air, he willingly complied. He pulled the truck to a halt under a big tree in the middle of the village square. As we staggered out more dead than alive, the air in the shadow was heavenly cool in contrast to the heat of the cabin. Again people swarmed around us. Children stared at me with curious big eyes but recoiled when I tried to touch them jokingly. A man in police uniform came up to us and spoke to the Father. He then turned to me. Could I please see a woman at the police station? She had tried to commit suicide and the police officer did not know what to do with her. I resigned myself to the fate of never getting a rest anywhere and followed him. The crowd of women and children swelled as we went across the square. They had to be pushed aside so I could enter the police station. In the darkness of the stuffy room I saw a sinister looking young woman with an unwilling, dull expression sitting in front of me. Through the noise of the curious people outside, I looked into her withdrawn face and asked, "Why did you chose to take your own life?" The woman looked at me with dark, expressionless eyes but did not answer. "Did your husband beat you?" She gave a slight nod. "Can't you return to your father's place?" She looked at me again, this time with

166

some surprise. Perhaps my knowledge of local customs brought us a little closer. "My husband will not let me go and I can't stand living with him, so what can I do? I have nothing to live for." Her voice was low and monotonous. "Don't you have any children?" She blew the air through her nose in contempt, "With that man!" She did not elaborate. "Does your husband not have other wives?" Again that surprised look. "No other woman would ever live with him," she said scornfully. "Could you not ask for a *baraza*, a village court hearing?" She shrugged her shoulders. "I would lose, of course. I have no rights, I am only a woman." Obviously she had given up. "What are you going to do then, when you get out of here?" I asked hesitantly. "Kill myself," she answered with a tired voice. She got up and turned away without looking at me and went into the cell with stooped shoulders and drooping head.

In the sweltering heat of the little office I tried to think out a solution to the problem. When I finally came out, some village elders had joined the crowd. "Unless you return this unhappy woman to her father and prevent her husband from taking her back, she is going to die." I spoke out loudly so everybody could hear what I said. I refused any discussion of the matter and returned to the shadow of the tree. By stating that the woman would die unless certain actions were taken and by avoiding mentioning her intention to kill herself, I had placed the responsibility for her life in the hands of the people. Up to now the neighbors of the desperate woman must have been rather indifferent to her suffering, but if she died now through suicide or otherwise, her death would be blamed on them for not having acted according to my suggestion.

There was no way I could take a rest in the shadow of the tree. People were jostling around me demanding my services. The Father was already seated, waiting for me in the truck. Only with great difficulty could I climb into the cabin. People looked at me with scorn when they realized I was getting away and angrily banged their fists against the sides of the truck as we slowly made our way through the crowd and drove on. The strain of all that had taken place on this day had exhausted me. I felt faint and utterly worn out. As I sat there dazed by the heat and fatigue, my thoughts could not find peace, even though I nearly dozed off. The arbitrary way in which things happen plagued my mind. Within such a short time span, I had played a part in two human tragedies. Regardless of my own feelings, they had presented themselves to me, naked and merciless as life itself, and I had been forced to act. First the sick man; he wanted to live and I was not able to help, yet his friends had thanked me with tearful eyes and warm handshakes. Then the depressed woman who wanted to die; I was able to help her, yet the people had not thanked me but had shown scornful eyes and clenched fists.

My weary mind went on working at such puzzles. When circumstances forced me to stay in the shadow of a tree without wanting to, I was not given a chance of saving a life, but when I was prevented from staying in the shadow of a tree although I wanted to, I was given the chance of saving a life.

It did not seem to make any sense.

18
My Medicine Man Colleague

The day had been long and the journey full of stressful events. With a sigh of relief, I at last caught sight of the mission at a turn of the road—it signaled a chance for rest and recovery. The mission station we were arriving at turned out to be a real outpost, recently established by a Swiss priest and his African helpers, and the living quarters were not much more than a cluster of mud huts. I happened to cast a glance into the dark smelly cove of a kitchen built on to one of the huts and when I put my head inside, a horde of cockroaches scurried in all directions, but I tried to forget about them when the friendly cook served the evening meal.

A mug of *Tembo* beer helped us overcome our apprehension, and soon the visiting Father and his host were eagerly discussing theology and their missionary activity. Most people in the Kilwa region were Moslems, the priest told us, and it was not easy to gain converts to Christianity. People viewed the newly established mission with suspicion, but they were thankful for the services offered: education and medical help for anyone who wanted it regardless of religion. However, the missionary, who had been trained as a teacher, soon found that it was mainly treatment for the sick the people wanted. He had therefore sent for me so that I could help him find a practical solution to his problem.

After we finished eating, we went outside to sit for a while in garden chairs and cool off in the evening air. The moon shone silvery through the branches of a small palm tree in front of the hut as the Fathers talked of their school days together in a Swiss seminary. The mission priest was speaking rapidly and working himself up into that excited state which in Africa is called "bush-happy." It occurs when one hits upon a sympathetic audience after having been alone in the bush for a long time. I knew it well myself. It starts slowly as a deep excitement, an inner quiver and increasing feeling of unreality. It is as if one part of oneself is standing outside looking at the self and trying to make it calm down and shut up before the situation gets too embarrassing. But pent up emotions and tension, accumulated through many frustrating experiences of everyday living with nobody to share them, surge to the surface and boil over in a stream of words which cannot be controlled. Those who have gone through this recognize it at once in others and feel obliged to listen patiently until the intensity of the experience wears off.

The moon went silently on its way among the stars and as I sat there, my limbs heavy from tiredness, the peaceful noises of the night mingled with the exalted voice of the lonely priest and I forgot to listen. . . . At long last the priest came to himself and jumped to his feet, suggesting that it was time to go to bed. Picking up the kerosene lamp from the doorway he turned to me with an embarrassed smile and asked me to follow him. We went across the yard to a small hut which stood alone in a clearing. "This is our humble guest house," the Father said somewhat apologetically, "You'll have to accept the modest comfort the mission can offer." I was too tired to notice even the small basin and the jug of water placed on a chair; I stumbled into bed and fell asleep.

It was pitch dark when I was startled awake. My heart was pounding and I lay stiff, listening in the dark. What had

170

awakened me? What was I hearing? There it was again; a peculiar noise outside. I tried to figure out what it was, but could not place the sound—like something boiling or like the rumbling of distant thunder. But it was close by and seemed to be moving around just outside the thin walls of my hut. Unable to identify the noise, I became increasingly alarmed. Maybe what I heard were the sinister doings of a witch doctor intent on scaring me away! In vain I strained my ears, but my own loud heart beats interfered with whatever I was hearing and I did not dare to get up and look outside. Then came the long drawn out howl of a hyena, a sound I knew well. It had the effect of interrupting the strange noise. I listened for a long time but could hear nothing unusual any more. It took me a while to fall asleep again. It was hot in the room and the bed was narrow and uncomfortable. It squeaked and I hardly dared to move lest somebody outside should know I was awake and listening. What a place to live in! I felt admiration for the priest who could stick it out here alone in the wilderness. I recalled him telling us that he would rid himself of his frustration and anger by throwing up, instead of getting angry at the people. Judging from his emaciated appearance, he must have had many opportunities to do so.

It was daylight when I opened my eyes again. I sat up quickly and was just getting out of bed when a cry of surprise slipped from my lips. Something like strange plants were standing in groups in front of the bed; long brown stalks, some more than a foot high, seemed to have grown out of the earthen floor during the night. As I was staring, a pale-colored ant appeared at the top of one of the pillars, carrying a lump of earth which it cemented on to the wall of the column. Then it disappeared inside and a second ant crawled forth with another lump. I relaxed and had to laugh; the funny stalks were the work of termites building their air shafts. They must have had their colony right underneath the floor of the hut. I knocked the earthen pillars down as I walked about doing my morning toilet. The funny sight put me into good spirits and made those inexplicable noises from the night seem less

171

frightening.

Much later, in conversation with a game warden I asked about those strange noises. To my surprise he started to laugh; he knew right away what I had heard. The rumbling sound of digestion in the intestines of elephants! These huge animals often use the quietness of night to graze around human habitation. Their soft broad soles tread so quietly that one would never suspect such giants to be around. When elephants relax, their digestion works and their intestines rumble. The noise can be heard at quite a distance. But the elephants can stop the noise at will and do so when they are startled. No wonder I had been unable to figure that out!

At that time, however, I was still concerned about the noise, and as a precaution against any adverse reactions to my arrival, I asked the missionary to send a messenger to all surrounding villages to announce to the people that *Mama Mganga* would like to speak to their elders and chiefs if they would do her the honor of coming to the mission for a meeting. While I was waiting for the men to arrive I checked through the modest equipment in the dispensary hut. I found the usual pots and jars with ointments, laxatives and worm remedies, as well as the ordinary drugs against malaria, colds, wound infections, indigestion, headaches and other common ailments. There was also a good supply of vitamins and iron tablets, medications which I could teach an interested and willing person how to use. The more sophisticated medicines which should be administered only by an experienced nurse or a physician I put in boxes and placed them in a corner for special use.

In the meantime the men were arriving. They greeted me with cool dignity and a certain curiosity. We sat down in a circle under a huge mango tree and I began by introducing myself and explaining why I had come to this place. The men did not look particularly friendly and I was nervous as I struggled along in Swahili telling them about my work as a doctor and wondering who might have disturbed me during the night. I looked them over carefully. I knew of certain tattoos and

172

ornaments which would reveal the medicine man among them. Then I spotted a chain with the typical medicine man badge around the neck of one, half-hidden under his shirt. This was one of the younger men in the group and when I caught his intelligent glance I felt he knew I had recognized him for what he was. But he did not blink. When I asked the men for an interpreter, since I did not know their tribal language and wanted to make sure I would understand all the patients, they nodded in approval and silently waited for what else I had to say. As I was going to be at the mission for only a short while, I asked them to choose one person interested in helping me and in learning how to use some of the medicines the mission could offer. There was a stir. They eagerly discussed this in their tribal language, which I could not understand. I observed them closely, however, and when I felt there was a certain indecision about whom to delegate for the job, I turned to the one I thought was a medicine man and asked him if he would be my helper. There was a tense silence. Surprise and bewilderment showed on all faces. But when, after some hesitation, the man agreed, the others burst out laughing, visibly impressed by my choice. I felt I had won the battle and, quickly, before the man had time to change his mind, I took him to the priest to settle the matter. The Father, happy about the prospect of having somebody trained to assist in the care of the sick, was pleased about the plan. He did not know the man, but seemed to find him trustworthy and they quickly agreed upon a small remuneration. The Father asked the thus established helper if he would consider taking further training as a dresser at the mission hospital in town. The medicine man replied with dignity that he would think about it after having tried out the job by helping *Mama Mganga* at the dispensary.

Quite excited about my new helper, I went with him to the dispensary where sick people were already waiting. He had not in any way indicated that he was a medicine man, but I was sure of it and thought about how to relate to him. I did not want to appear as the all-knowing teacher who doles out wisdom to an inexperienced pupil. I was sure this man knew

173

everybody who came to the dispensary, and that he had already treated most of them at one time or the other. I saw how the patients' eyes widened with surprise, and probably also fear, when they realized who was my helper. But they kept their thoughts to themselves and flocked to the dispensary as usual. During the first few days I was too busy to give my new helper much attention, but I noticed that he was keenly observing and listening, while translating for me. During work I therefore made it a habit to comment on what I was doing as if talking to myself, and to explain why I arrived at a diagnosis and how I used various drugs. I had the embarrassing feeling that the medicine man found my treatment methods rather unsophisticated, which was indeed true, due to the poorly equipped dispensary and the few medicines I had at my disposal.

Most patients suffered from malaria, which is easily treated with modern Western drugs and after a few days on antimalaria medication, they improved considerably. But if the medicine man was impressed with my results, he did not show it and I began to feel uneasy with his lack of response. However, this changed dramatically one day after an unexpected event. A young woman who had already been treated for malaria returned with her family. They were concerned because she still felt extremely weak. The woman was severely anemic and I decided to give her an intra-muscular injection of vitamins. I told the family that she would be given a powerful medicine and looked through the boxes I had set aside. I do not know whether the vitamin ampoules had been stored away too long in the hot climate, or what was wrong with them, but as I was handling the vial it suddenly exploded in my hands, scattering glass and liquid about. Most of it hit me, but apart from soiling my clothes, did not do any harm. But the people were scared stiff. They stood stunned while I calmly cleaned up the mess. Trembling with fear, they assured me that the sick woman felt much better already and did not really need any more medicine. Hastily they left the dispensary. I glanced with embarrassment at my helper who had a big grin on his face. With admiration in his voice he said. "That was powerful medicine indeed!" The ice was broken and we began to exchange views regarding illnesses and their treatment.

Our concepts of health and disease were quite different, but the medicine man was willing to accept my therapies if he could explain their effectiveness according to his own theories. To him, most abdominal pains were due to a *nyoka*, a snake nesting there. People with severe malaria attacks often have abdominal pains due to swelling of the spleen. When the malaria is treated the swelling goes down and the pain disappears. To my helper, this meant that the medicine had killed that *nyoka* in the patient's abdomen. There were other times when I learned from the medicine man. It had been raining heavily for a few days, when finally the sun reappeared and dried up the damp ground. Towards evening that day a youngster was brought to the dispensary suffering from severe abdominal pain. The poor boy was doubled up and pressed his hands against his stomach crying in distress. Finding nothing but distended bowels, I concluded that he was seriously constipated and wanted to give him a laxative. My helper who had watched me asked the boy's friends a few questions. Then he turned to me. "*Mama Mganga*, this is something you probably have never heard about before," he said apologetically. "Let me explain it to you before you give the medicine. The rainy season is the time when the termites swarm, especially after a heavy rainfall like we just had. The boys know this and watch the termite hills early in the morning. When the sun begins to warm up the ant hill a queen will come out, spread her wings and fly up into the air on her way to found a new colony. The winged termites which we call *kumbikumbi* swarm out behind her and at the moment of taking off they are caught in bags by the children. *Kumbikumbi* termites are one of our favorite delicacies. The women will fry the soft fat insects over the fire, shaking them well and discarding the wings which fall off. But the hungry children do not wait for the frying; they eat the *kumbikumbi* on the spot, wings and all. Sometimes they eat too many and then the wings of the insects lump together in the belly, blocking the passage. That is what happened to this boy. Giving laxatives by mouth has never helped to move the lump of wings; one has to get at it from the other end.''

I could see he was right; the chitin of the insects' wings would lead to bowel obstruction in the lower parts of the intestines. But how could we give the lad an enema? The dispensary did not have the necessary utensils. ''Just wait a minute,'' said the medicine man. He took a knife and went into the bush. After a while he returned with a green bamboo shoot. It was hollow and soft. With that ingenious piece of equipment we went to work, aided by the boys and other concerned people. Everybody waited anxiously for the enema to work, knowing that it was a matter of extreme urgency for the poor boy who continued to whimper with pain. When finally a myriad of termite wings came out in a gush of water, people jumped up and down and laughed with joy and relief. They teased the embarrassed boy and made jokes until he got up and joined the others with a smile, now feeling well again. Everybody thanked my helper for the clever way he had solved the problem.

The extremely hot and humid climate on the coast caused people to suffer attacks of tropical malaria with exceptionally severe fever delirium, hallucinations and mental confusion. One day a young man was brought to us in such a delirious state, which prompted the medicine man to tell me his theories in regard to mental disturbances. I had given the raving man antimalaria medicine and tranquilizers and while we were watching him slowly calm down, my helper told me in a low voice, ''We used to think that madness was caused by revengeful ancestral spirits, or by a sorcerer's poison, but nowadays we know other causes. This man is deranged because he is possessed by a *shetani*.'' The medicine man placed my hands on the patient's feet. ''Do you feel how cold they are? The *shetani* makes the blood stop moving; that's why the patient cries out and talks nonsense. The *shetani* sits in his limbs and makes the body shiver.'' Suppose the medicine man's concept

176

of *shetani* could be equated with my concept of the malaria parasite, our etiological theories would be pretty much the same, I thought. "What do you mean by *shetani*?" I asked after a pause. "*Shetanis* are foreign Devils," he explained, "evil spirits coming to this country with foreigners from Arabia, Asia or Europe. As many peoples now travel to the cities, they come in contact with foreigners and might pick up a *shetani* from them. When people return home, the *shetani* comes along. That's why there are more disturbed people in our villages than before. Sometimes the *shetani* will show itself in a dream; it talks to the possessed or speaks through his mouth. Only a medicine man is able to understand that kind of talk and to recognize what sort of *shetani* is plaguing the patient. Medicine men can prepare remedies out of roots, barks and herbs, which have the power to drive out the evil foreign spirit once it has been identified."

I wondered whether my helper was going to suggest using some of his remedies on this patient, and I did not want to offend him by refusing so I said that since the patient was now soundly asleep with my medicine, we should wait a day or two before trying anything else. The medicine man agreed, and as the fever receded during the night and the patient regained the senses towards the next evening, my helper graciously admitted that my European medicine had cured the madness this time. "I guess the *shetani* was a European one," he concluded with his infallible logic.

As the days passed we worked increasingly well together. I had to admire my conscientious helper, who would never undertake treatment before he felt completely confident that he understood and knew what he was doing. To my regret, however, I never could get him to pull teeth. No wonder! Even dentists in their modern offices are sometimes nervous when extracting a tooth. How much more reason for caution there in the bush with instruments so old-fashioned they would be museum pieces elsewhere and with no anesthesia except for a few aspirins. To extract a tooth under such circumstances, sometimes in a person with an inflamed jaw, extremely painful even to touch, was one of the most nerve-racking and dreaded jobs I had to perform. But people would rather go through the pains of extraction than be sent back home with their aching tooth. Locked jaws, abscesses and open sores all testified to the agony people suffered when no dental care was available. Some of the missionaries had acquired a special skill in pulling teeth and since it often required a man's strength to remove a reticent tooth, I was always relieved when there was a Father available willing to take on this unpleasant task. Since the priest of this outpost mission had no inclination to do that kind of job, I kept hoping that no patient with toothache would turn up. Sometimes penicillin and aspirin would spare both patient and myself the painful procedure. But my hopes were idle. One day a man presented himself at the dispensary and I had to admit that extraction was the only solution to his painful problem.

The awful feeling of tension in the stomach and the trembling hands which I always experienced when I had to inflict pain on a patient gripped me as I dug out the rusty old dental pliers and cleaned them in preparation for the operation. I gave the moaning patient as many aspirin tablets as I thought he could tolerate and when his toothache was dulled, sat him outside under a tree. He folded his hands on the back of a chair and anchored his feet around its legs. My helper stood behind the patient and held the man's head firmly between his hands. The sick tooth was the last lower molar and as I carefully chose the right tongs, the patient gave a big sigh, closed his eyes and courageously opened his mouth. I mustered all my strength, took a deep breath and began to pull. I could feel all the muscles in the patient's body tighten; he opened his eyes wide and sweat appeared on his forehead. "Think you are pulling out a cork from a wine bottle," a dentist once told me while demonstrating the manipulations used for extraction. Remembering his words, I applied increasing force to the tooth. Once I started to pull, I tried not to give in until the tooth was out, as this seemed to be the least painful for the patient. But alas, this time it did not work. The bad tooth refused to budge. Bathed in sweat I had to take a break. When I made another attempt to get the tooth out, the poor man could not help letting out cries of torment. I struggled with the forceps and pulled with all my might; there was an awful noise as if I was about to crack his jaw, and the man roared with pain.

At that moment the visiting Father rushed out to see what was happening. I was out of breath and the crowd of people which had accumulated around the gruesome scene were voicing their disappointment while the poor man's tooth ached more than ever. I moistened my lips, and swallowed a few times. "Father, I think this is a job for a man," I said and handed him the pair of tongs. "Sure, I know how to pull teeth." The Father looked as calm as ever. With a nonchalant gesture he took the instrument and busied himself with it. Before the patient even had time to feel the pain, the Father triumphantly held up the bloody tooth in the grip of the tongs. The people cheered and applauded. Even the patient who had been sitting in a daze finally had to smile. We gave him water to rinse his aching mouth and when he had recovered a bit, I asked him to open it again as I was concerned I might have injured his jaw with my manipulations. Wiping off the blood, I suddenly felt hot and cold. Oh no! The Father had pulled the wrong tooth! Consternation nearly made me drop to the ground as I stared at the bad tooth sitting there in the innermost corner beside the gaping wound, just as firmly as before. I did not have the heart to tell the patient; he could not possibly have endured more pain at this time. I decided to reveal nothing about my embarrassing discovery, but have the patient come again after a few days. In the meantime he was to take penicillin and other drugs to heal the wound. With mixed feelings I saw the man leaving with his friends and heard them joke about the loud cries he had produced. I felt angry at the Father, but since I had not mastered the situation myself, I did not feel I could blame him for what had happened. As the patient never returned for further treatment, I felt awfully guilty about the whole affair.

I had not quite recovered from this event when a young woman who had just given birth came down with a bad toothache. I examined her and saw to my dismay that I would have to take out the tooth. The woman looked at me with a tired expression and whispered, "Please *Mama Mganga* don't hurt me. I just can't take any more pain." I combed through all the available supplies of medicines which I had tucked away. Many of them consisted of small physician's samples distributed by pharmaceutical companies in Europe and sent on to the missions in Africa. Many were useless, either because the supply was too small, or because the illness for which they were intended did not occur in the tropics. But this time I found a small vial of an anesthetic for dental purposes. I carefully injected the precious drug into the gum, waited for a while and when I extracted the tooth the woman did not even notice that I had already pulled it out. She stared incredulously at the bloody tooth, and then she grasped my hand and thanked me profoundly. The next morning a group of people waited for me when I came out of my hut. They looked at me with eyes full of expectation. What did they want? "*Mama Mganga*, we all want to feel how it is to have a tooth pulled without any pain."

I decided it was time for me to leave! When my things had been packed and the truck stood ready for departure, the medicine man, who had been such a faithful helper, and who now would have to carry on alone, stepped up to me. He looked at me and said in a confidential tone, "*Mama Mganga* I went to see the man who had his tooth pulled by the Father." A smile flitted across his face when he noticed my uneasiness and he continued, "I helped him to get rid of another tooth beside the first one pulled, as it had also started to ache. It came out easily and now he has no pain any more." I saw a twinkle in his eyes as I thanked him. We did not talk any more about the matter. I think he was satisfied by my sigh of relief as I climbed into the truck. He was surely one of the most tactful colleagues I have ever known.

19
The Maskini Boy

Whenever I had the opportunity to work at one of the missions situated in the Mahenge mountains, I felt great relief, not only because of the cool fresh air at night, but because there were always one or two nurses among the many nuns stationed at the Kwiro mission. This gave me some free time since the nurse and her helpers could take care of the dispensary. Calling upon me only for difficult cases, they could look after some of the patients in the small treatment room until I had time to see them.

I loved to go for walks in the mountains and enjoy the scenery before me, overlook the plains below and see the little villages half hidden among the banana groves. The people working in the fields smiled and greeted me as I passed by and the little children came running from the huts to follow me at a distance. I would hear them giggle and whisper behind my back. When I turned around to face them, they would run away laughing but scared at the same time. As I went along the path I would meet men coming home from hunting, bow and arrows in hand, women with their babies on their backs returning from the fields and old women carrying heavy loads of firewood on their heads. I had to admire the physical strength of these fragile looking old women. I once tried to lift their load myself and I was hardly able to place it on my head. After a few steps I had to put the heavy burden down, much to the old women's amusement.

Fields of manioc and millet alternated with landscapes of huge black rocks of fantastic shape where hardly anything but grass and cactus would grow. And then there were mountain streams with lush vegetation along the banks, forgotten coffee plantations long ago cultivated by German planters of the past, with beautiful flowers and trees, not to mention gracious birds of delightful shapes and colors such as I had never seen before. There were unfamiliar smells and noises and at times the frightening experience of hearing animals prowling in the thick underbrush without being able to see them. And above the trees the tropical sun brightening the colors and dazzling the senses.

Once I lost my way among the rocks and trees. I turned a few times on the narrow path and tried to find my way back, but my orientation was gone. Slowly the blissful feeling of being amidst warm and friendly nature gave way to an increasing apprehension. Sunset was nearing and I had been warned that hungry leopards were out looking for prey at dusk. With pounding heart I thought I saw their spotted fur between the trees and behind the rocks. A big black snake appeared on the road and came gliding down the path toward me. I stood motionless, paralyzed. The snake came slowly closer; it seemed to look me directly in the eyes and showed no fear or hurry. Just in front of me it suddenly turned off the road and disappeared into the bush. The majestic tranquility of that snake made a tremendous impact on me, and as I stood there recovering from the shock, I perceived a person hidden among the trees looking at me from some distance. Realizing I had seen him, the person came hesitantly out of the bush. Glad to have found another human being, I hurried towards him, but noticing his fear I slowed my steps. He was a strange sight.

Seemingly a young boy, he had the face of an old man. His expression was humble and mild but also curious and shy as he glanced at me. He looked filthy and neglected and old rags barely covered parts of his body. His skin was wrinkled, dry and cracked, especially on the legs, as one sees it in severely undernourished people and his arms showed thick keloid scars from poorly healed wounds. Flies seemed glued to his body and lumps of dirt stuck to his skin. Behind him I noticed a small ramshackle hut. I felt a spontaneous sympathy for the strange boy.

"Are you living here all alone?" I asked in amazement. "Good afternoon *Memsahib*," answered the boy with a dry crackling voice; he was not lacking good manners, but did not say another word, only stood there as if waiting. "I have lost my way, can you show me how to get back to the mission?" I asked. He nodded and started to walk along the path. After a while, he turned his head to make sure I followed, but kept at a distance which made conversation impossible. After we had walked for a while he stopped and with a humble gesture indicated that he wanted to carry my bag. When I declined he looked so disappointed that I gave it to him anyway. He placed it on his head and walked on ahead of me with stiff, clumsy movements. I thought his thin neck would bend under the rather heavy bag, but he marched on unperturbed. As soon as we approached the first settlement he stopped, put down the load and whispered in his strange voice, "Goodbye, *Mama Mganga*," then he quickly ran back into the forest. "Who was this boy?" I asked a young woman who was pounding maize in the yard and had seen us coming. She shrugged her shoulders indifferently and as I persisted she explained with some contempt in her voice, "Just a *maskini*."

My heart sank; that placed the boy in the category of a social outcast. *Maskini* means the poor one; the wretched one who through illness, old age or other misfortune has lost his capacity to act as a useful member of society; the useless one who has no productive function. A *maskini* has no duties any more; he is unable to take the responsibility of keeping himself alive and must be given food and shelter. Families usually look after their own *maskini*, but if they misbehave they can be chased away. A person who has been labelled a *maskini* must behave in a certain way. He must be utterly humble and unobtrusive; he cannot take part in any conversation or join the people around the fire unless invited. Usually the *maskini* sits quietly in a corner or somewhere apart from the others, living on the crumbs left over for him. Quietly and without protest he must tolerate all kinds of abuse people might heap on him. He is a beggar without any property, privileges or rights in his society, living at the mercy of others. Once a *maskini* he is beyond blame and arouses no other feelings than contempt or pity.

I felt very sad for the boy, and while I hurried back to the mission I pondered about why this boy was a *maskini*, and why he was living alone in the forest since *maskini* usually stay at some hidden place in the villages. Except for some wounds and scars on his body and his clumsy movements, he did not look physically ill and mentally he appeared alert and normal. But he obviously avoided contact with other people. Perhaps the aged expression on his face was due to the hardship of his existence as a social outcast. What could be the matter with him? For days I could not forget the impression he had made upon me with his humble and mysterious silence and his old-young face.

Some days went by until I again found time for a stroll in the mountains. This time I did not venture far and chose a path in another direction. To my great surprise I again met the *maskini* boy on a lonely part of the road. From then on I would meet him every time I went for a walk, no matter how far apart the places were. How on earth could he know where I would go and when I would take a walk? It seemed weird and I would have been scared had it not been for his unaggressive and humble behavior. There he was, always keeping his distance, hardly speaking a word except for a greeting, disappearing in the bush as soon as anybody else came along or when we came close to a village, always reappearing as soon

184

as everybody was gone. He showed his friendly inclination in many small ways, leading me to beautiful places and pointing out to me birds and animals which I would never have noticed without his keen eyes. Strange it was to know nothing of his life and still to feel his kindness. Whenever I tried to make some personal contact he became anxious and unhappy and never answered my questions. Sometimes I sat down to eat and offered him some food. Then his face lit up and he reached for it with trembling hands, saliva running from his mouth. His face continued to fascinate me and one day I brought along my charcoal pencil and paper and asked if he would allow me to draw his portrait. I do not think he understood what I meant, but he sat quietly looking straight ahead while I did the drawing. The only time I saw him smile was when I showed him the finished portrait, but even then he did not say a word. Who knows what he was thinking! There were days or even weeks when I had no time for hikes in the mountains but whenever I ventured out alone, that strange boy, the *maskini*, was at hand.

On Sundays I sometimes attended Mass at the mission. I liked to see the people gathered in their best clothes, the women with the curious and smiling little children on their backs. One Sunday during the service a terrible cry rang through the church. It sounded like the cry of a dying person and terrified the people. Panic-striken they rushed for the doors. The children screamed with fear as they squeezed through the doorways, but I remained in my seat, fearing the stampeding masses more than whoever had caused the turmoil. Finally everybody was outside and in the silence of the deserted church I heard some strange noises coming from a dark corner. I went over and found my friend the *maskini* writhing in convulsions. That was what was wrong with him. The poor boy was an epileptic and while hiding in a corner of the church a sudden epileptic attack had thrown him to the floor. I helped him as best I could and when the convulsions had quietened down I got some people to carry the unconscious boy to our dispensary where I gave him an anticonvulsive injection. After about half an hour the boy came to his senses. When he looked up and saw me and the nurse, he understood that we had watched him having an epileptic seizure. His eyes widened with fear. He jumped to his feet and before we got over our amazement, he staggered down the road and disappeared from our view.

After that, the *maskini* did not turn up to accompany me on my walks in the mountains anymore. The nurse then told me that people dreaded epileptics and believed an evil spirit possesses the convulsing person, hence the panic in the church. Those afflicted are deeply ashamed of their condition and accept social isolation as a matter of course. I could now understand the boy's behavior and feelings and I decided that I would try to help him. I took with me a small bottle with phenobarbital tablets, a well known anticonvulsive medication, and went to the place where I had first met the boy. It took me a long time to find the spot where I had encountered the snake and I proceeded cautiously lest I should come upon the creature unawares. But everything remained quiet in the hot mid-day sun and finally I saw the little hut among the trees. I called the boy, but he did not come out. "Don't be afraid of me, maybe I can help you." No answer. Had the timid youngster left for good?" His desolate hut appeared to be empty, but I slowly approached and found him crouched behind his little garden, hiding from view as best he could. "Listen, my friend," I said gently, "I know the illness you have and I am not afraid of it. Come here, I have a medicine with me which will take away your attacks." But the boy did not move or raise his eyes. I sat down beside him and saw his quivering mouth and tears running from his lowered eyes. He looked so miserable I would have liked to take him in my arms but I did not want to scare him away. I spoke to him for a long time, telling him that I could see no reason for him to feel embarrassed. In my eyes it was not his fault that he had fallen ill. Finally I placed the container with the little white tablets in front of him and told him to take one every evening before going to sleep. He stared at the medicine and his body started to tremble, but he still did not move or say a word. "Will you take the medicine?" I asked and waited until he hesitatingly nodded his head. I left some food with him and said I would come again in a couple of weeks.

Two weeks later I returned with more food and medicine. This time the boy came forth. He grasped my hand and said in his crackling voice, *"Mama Mganga*, I have not had any more seizures." He eagerly received his supply of medicine for another two weeks. From then on he greeted me with a smile and a new air of hope lit up his face. I noticed that he was keeping himself clean and that he had thatched the roof of his little hut and worked his garden. The whole place looked friendlier and when he now accompanied me, he would begin to respond to my questions. It took many walks before I was able to piece together his tragic life story.

As a little boy he lived with his parents in a village not far from the mission. He was the youngest of three brothers, but as he was bright and eager to learn, the parents decided to let him go to school at the mission. Competition for admission to this school was stiff and many dismal parents had to return home with their weeping children who failed the entrance examination. However, the boy learned English quickly and got into second grade without difficulties. His mother felt so proud and happy, she forgot the old peoples' advice never to brag about one's children and praised her clever son in front of her neighbors. Too late she saw jealousy in the eyes of a neighboring woman whose son had been rejected at the same school. Frightened, she returned home, not daring to mention what had happened.

One day the boy was alone at home studying. The neighbor woman entered. She went up to the boy and pressed her hands against his head. The frightened boy heard her mutter some words and her hands felt like a burning ring around his head. The woman looked into his eyes and said, "Poor boy, you will soon be sick and have fits." Then she hurried out. When his mother came home she found her son huddling in a corner, trembling and sobbing from fear. The boy told her what had occurred and the whole family became apprehensive and fearful of what was going to happen. A few days later the boy had his first epileptic seizure, and everybody was convinced that the neighbor woman had used magic poison on him. But hoping that there would not be any more attacks and wanting to keep the shameful event secret they decided to take no action against her, and the boy returned to school as if nothing had happened. Unfortunately he had his second attack right in the middle of the classroom. The children fled in terror and even the African teacher left the room. When the boy came to himself he was alone in the school and cried bitterly, knowing too well that the news about his disease would spread to all the villages where the schoolchildren lived. Still he went back to school the next day, but the teacher told him to stay away. The children looked at him as if he were a dangerous being. Not even his closest friends would put in a word for him. As he stood there forsaken, the teacher told him to go home and that if he turned up again the parents of the other children would forbid them to attend school. The boy realized that he had no chance and, discouraged, he went home.

In the beginning of his illness the family was supportive and tried to make up for his misfortune, but as his attacks became more frequent they felt embarrassed and afraid. Since it was the general belief that the evil spirit which possesses the epileptic might jump over to any bystander during a seizure, or be transmitted by the saliva frothing from the mouth and by the urine going off, not even his mother would dare to stay with him and help him. It happened therefore that he burned himself on an open fire during a fit, left alone as he was. His father took him to a medicine man but the old man shook his head and said it was too late to help as the boy already had burns on his body. Embittered, the father called a *baraza*, a village court, and accused the neighbor woman of witchcraft. She was called in front of all the elders at the *baraza* to defend herself. She, of course, denied having harmed the boy and said she had heard the boy cry and went over to see what was the matter. There were no other witnesses and with only the poor

188

boy's words against hers, she was acquitted.

Now friends and neighbors started to avoid the family. The boy's younger sisters cried if he wanted to play with them and his brothers, afraid that he might have a seizure, did not take him along on their excursions any more. When he sometimes hit them in frustration, he was severely punished by his parents. He was told never to touch another person; his food was prepared in separate dishes and he had to fetch his own water from a waterhole far away. Even at night he had to stay away from the others and sleep alone close to the door. With growing grief he realized how everybody, even his mother, avoided his company. Soon his parents started to call him *maskini* and used a harsher voice when talking to him than when speaking to the other children. He tried to rebel and the parents finally decided that he had to leave the home. His father knew of an old abandoned hut in the forest. That was where he would have to live. His mother wept when they accompanied him to the lonely place and she helped him plant a small garden while his father repaired the hut. The boy remembered how desperately frightened he was when he found himself abandoned there in the forest. In the beginning he would run home when fear overwhelmed him, but each time he turned up at home his parents became increasingly annoyed and took him back to his lonely abode. His father warned him not to come close to the village. Anyone knowing that he was an epileptic possessed by evil spirits could stone him, chase him away or even kill him.

During his first year in the bush his mother would visit him or persuade one of his brothers to bring him some food, but then visits became less and less frequent and he had to spend most of his time in solitude struggling for survival as best he could. He seldom dared to make a fire or venture far away from his hut lest he would have an attack. His life became burdensome, but fatigue and hunger dulled his senses. As there was nothing to look forward to he became depressed and resigned himself to his wretched existence, only awaiting the day when he would succumb to some illness or drown or burn to death in an attack. His only comfort had been to hide in a corner of the church, listening to the music and ceremony of the Sunday mass.

In spite of the fact that on medication he had no further attacks, the boy remained depressed and withdrawn. My suggestion that he might return home now that he was free of seizures only aroused apprehension and renewed fear. I thought about a way of getting him out of his fatalistic apathy.

One day when he appeared in a good mood I told him that, encouraged by the good recovery he had made, I wanted to start a treatment center for epileptics. I would offer the medication he was receiving to any epileptic who wanted to be treated. I told him that I needed a helper who could speak English well and who knew the local people, their customs and their language. Since he himself had experienced both the illness and its treatment, and as I considered him a clever boy, I thought he would be well-suited for such a job. The boy was silent for a long time. It was moving to observe how his face reflected conflicting feelings of hope and fear. "Then I would not be a *maskini* any more," he whispered, and after a little while he added, "I would be able to go home." I could see his anxiety mount as he wondered whether or not they would accept him at home and I quickly added, "If you will be my helper you will receive a small salary, and for the time being I would prefer that you stay at the mission so that you could be available all the time." The boy seemed to grow. He stood up. A new dignity shone in his eyes. "All right, *Mama Mganga*, I accept." He looked me straight in the face and with a faint smile he said, "You help me by letting me help you."

20
A Treatment Center for Kifafa

The Swahili word for epilepsy is *kifafa*. *Kifa* means "to die," and the repetition of a syllable is diminutive, therefore *kifafa*, little dying. An epileptic having a seizure, falling down with a cry, writhing with convulsions, froth flowing from his mouth, and then lying unconscious on the ground, does indeed look like a dying person. Seeing the tortured expression on the face of the convulsing person and how he is helplessly thrown around, the people of the mountains among whom I worked were convinced that a powerful spirit took possession of the *kifafa* victim. They also feared that the same spirit might jump from the afflicted person to anybody close by. Anyone who came in contact with the saliva or the excrements of the epileptic would be endangered. Therefore, everybody would run away instead of protecting and helping the convulsing person who, deeply unconscious during an attack, could so easily hurt himself.

Kifafa is looked upon not only with fear but also with shame. It is a disgrace to the entire family and is believed to be caused by witchcraft or to be the punishment for certain misdeeds of the afflicted himself or of his kin. The parents' quarrel might lead to *kifafa* in their child, or if a mother is unfaithful during the time of pregnancy, she or her child might become epileptic. Breaking the taboos, alcohol abuse, laziness or other vices incur ancestors' wrath. They might punish the family by sending the evil spirit of *kifafa*.

People know the difference between ordinary fever convulsions of little children and the onset of the *kifafa* illness and they have many rules, especially for children, for how to avoid becoming an epileptic. In a fight one should not strike the other on the head; children should avoid spinning around so that they will not get dizzy, as this is a symptom of *kifafa*; the fish-eagle must not be hunted because when it is swooping down upon its prey it drops to earth like an epileptic falling to the ground in an attack. A child should not kill a fowl by cutting its neck or watch anybody else doing so, because a decapitated bird jerks just like an epileptic. An epileptic must not even eat a bird thus killed unless a medicine man has given him a root to cook with it.

Encouraged by the surprising recovery of my young epileptic assistant, I wanted to extend the anticonvulsive treatment to other epileptics, but when I began to show an interest in patients suffering from *kifafa*, the people's attitude toward me changed. As soon as I asked about this illness, the usually friendly people of the mountains became withdrawn and apprehensive. The people's fear of *kifafa* was such that nobody dared to talk about it. Discussing *kifafa* with a stranger could provoke the spirit's anger. People hid their *kifafa* sufferers from me and would not believe that I could possibly control the evil spirit with small white tablets. I soon realized that I would get nowhere with my enquiries and decided to try a different approach.

For years the mission had sheltered *maskinis* and I noticed that most of these people hanging around the mission doing all kinds of small jobs in return for food and shelter were actually suffering from *kifafa*. About a dozen such women lived in a small house close to the vegetable garden. A kind-hearted old nun looked after them, helping them when

192

they had convulsions and encouraging them to do gardening with her when they felt up to it. The mission brother who attended the cattle cared for a similar flock of epileptic men. Living close to the stable, they helped him in his daily chores. Although the men often had violent quarrels among themselves, they all loved the friendly brother who helped them as best he could. I decided to start my treatment of epilepsy with these patients. If I was successful it would become known that even such severely handicapped people can be helped and other *kifafa* sufferers might be brought to me for treatment.

I remember well my first visit to the epileptic men down by the stable. There were about fourteen of them. These men were plagued by convulsive fits day and night. One hefty young man used to spin round and round before falling down in convulsions; another ran around wildly not aware of where he went and whom he met. When he finally came to his senses he would find himself miles away with bleeding feet somewhere in the bush. What strange and pitiful figures they were! Full of sores, with burns and scars, some with crippled hands and feet, some lame, others half blind, some mentally dull, others nervous and shaking. One young boy practically lived in a flour-sack. He crept into it, tightened it firmly around his neck and rolled on the ground, gnashing the red earth between his teeth. I had been warned that some of the men might suddenly be seized with anger and lash out at anybody close enough to be hit. As they came slowly forward and stood around me in a semicircle, looking at me with their swollen, distorted and mask-like faces, I felt fearful and did not know what to say to them. An old man among them with incredibly spindly legs and staggering gait, stepped in front of the others, folded his hands and said in a thin voice "Let us thank *Mungu* [God] that he has sent *Mama Mganga* to us, and pray that He will help us to get rid of the evil spirit of *kifafa*." They all folded their hands as best they could and spoke in unison. Their simple prayer nearly moved me to tears and certainly took away any apprehension I had felt. One of them, a young boy with a withered arm, rolled a log in front of me with his

193

foot and proudly invited me to sit down. I took out a booklet in which I noted down all their names, showed them the medicine and began to organize a treatment plan with them. We all agreed that the old man should be their leader. They should report all their attacks and other symptoms to him. On my visit once a week he would let me know what had happened. I would note it down in my book and keep track of their improvement. The old man would also be responsible for keeping their weekly supply of medicine and dispensing it every day according to my orders. If one of them should need urgent help, he was to fetch me from the dispensary and I would come immediately. They nodded in silence, knowing all too well that they could not go to the dispensary like ordinary people; their presence would be too objectionable to the other patients.

During the first few weeks of the treatment program I went around feeling tense and nervous about this venture. These patients not only suffered from epilepsy but from all kinds of concomitant diseases and I neither had a hospital close by nor any equipment to make the necessary investigations. I also worried that when the attacks were suppressed, other aspects of the illness might become more prominent, for example mood disturbance or mental disorder. What if they forgot to take their medicine? A series of violent convulsive attacks sometimes ending in death could ensue. But as the weeks passed and nothing happened, I began to enjoy my visits to these patients. It was such a delight to see these once so depressed and miserable people now coming to greet me with smiles, proudly showing me the work they had done and announcing that they had not had any more attacks for a long time. Some of them came to visit me at the dispensary, despite the other patients' apprehension, just to tell me they had not forgotten to take their medicine and to proudly show off their new healthy appearance. The other patients seemed at first surprised and then increasingly curious about my treatment of these *kifafa* sufferers. When some of the younger epileptics dared to return to their villages and were accepted by their families, word spread among the people that *Mama Mganga* indeed could defeat the *kifafa* spirit with the little white pills. Soon epileptics from far and near embarked on a pilgrimage to the mission. Contrary to their usual concern for sick relatives, families would bring their *kifafa* sufferers to the mission during the night and abandon them outside my quarters. I would find them in the morning when I opened my door, half starved and covered with filth and sores. They would be lying on the ground in their wet and dirty rags, shivering with cold and fear. Overwhelmed by embarrassment and timidity they hardly dared to move. I literally had to lift them up and drag them indoors.

Because of the other people's fear I could not take the *kifafa* patients to the dispensary and saw no other solution than to examine them in my own room. Soon my quarters would buzz with the flies which always seemed to thrive on these poor wretches. The smell of poverty and illness would hang on in the room long after the patients had left. Every morning the same thing happened and soon the facilities at the mission were overcrowded. I discussed the situation with my epileptic helper. We decided that he would have to tell the people that unless the family came along and was willing to assume responsibility for their epileptic member, I would refuse to treat him. I had to steel myself and leave the abandoned epileptics unattended outside my door for a few days until the relatives, reluctantly at first, stayed with the patient. I noticed that the *kifafa* patients were markedly intimidated by the presence of family members. Had they been mumbling a few answers to my inquiries before, they would now give up completely. Crouching humbly on the floor, they left the answering to their relatives. If I addressed a question directly to the patient he would look anxiously at his relatives and only if they gave permission would he whisper a reply.

It was heart breaking to observe how rudely these usually gentle people treated their relatives with *kifafa*. It must have been the unconquerable fear of the *kifafa* spirit which dictated such behaviour, and also the fact that it was a disaster for the whole family to have one of them ill with *kifafa*. Even the healthy young people of such a family hardly had any chance of making a good match when of marriageable age. Sisters of an epileptic cannot secure the usually high bridal price and brothers will be denied brides from healthy families. The epileptics themselves have few chances to get married at all unless their condition is unknown or concealed at the time of marriage. Should their illness become manifest, the afflicted are subjected to extremely rough handling and abuse if not outright rejection by the partner's family. Sometimes two epileptics will live together and share their miserable lot, trying to help each other and keeping each other company. Children born from such a union will be taken from the parents and cared for by relatives, unless the child should turn out to be sick, too. Then it is left with the epileptic parents but has few chances of survival.

Among the many *kifafa* patients there was a man who caught my special interest. He was not at all downtrodden and depressed like the others but, on the contrary, seemed to demand respect from those around him. He had at least two seizures every month, and there was no doubt that he suffered from *kifafa*. But in spite of this he always came by himself and behaved with self-assurance and dignity even among non-*kifafa* patients. Some of the younger people would kneel down and keep their eyes on the floor when he spoke to them. I noticed that people avoided eye contact with this man and I wondered why until one day I met him outside the mission. Unaware of my presence he came walking along the road. He seemed deeply preoccupied and looked at the stony path as he approached. Just as we passed each other he happened to look up. Our eyes met and something like an electric current went through me. I nearly stumbled and turned around to greet him. But he continued on his way unperturbed and I was convinced he had not even recognized me. I could not explain what had happened, but I now understood why people were afraid of his look. Speaking with him when he came for treatment, I never experienced that startling sensation again, but was now even more interested in him than before. He had been under my treatment for about three months when one day he waited until everybody else had left the dispensary. He asked me in a low voice if he could come to see me early next morning before everybody else. I consented, curious about what he wanted.

Before sunrise he knocked at my door. Somewhat surprised I hurriedly got dressed and opened the door. Draped in a colorful blanket with a chain around his neck, a strange head dress, paint on his face, a large bundle in one hand and a Chief's cane in the other, he looked impressively dignified as he entered. He went straight to the window, closed it, pulled the curtains and placed the cane against the door. When this was done he turned to me and addressed me in a very solemn voice, "*Mama Mganga*, I have not told you before but I am also a *mganga*. I have treated many people suffering from *kifafa*, but I could not cure myself nor could any of the other medicine men I asked for help. I know your medicine works. It has cured many people and I myself have not had any more seizures since you started the treatment. I cannot thank you enough for what you are doing for me and for my people. I hear you asking people about their beliefs and fears regarding *kifafa*. Because I feel your interest is genuine I want to share with you some of my knowledge." I watched breathlessly as he began to untie his bundle. This was the first time I was face to face with an African medicine man who revealed himself to me so forthrightly. He now opened his bundle which contained many kinds of roots, bark and leaves. A pungent odor filled the room. I kept silent but sensing my keen interest, he sat down beside his bundle and spread the cloth on the floor. Carefully arranging the various ingredients in a certain order he began to talk. "My father was a famous medicine man. He inherited knowledge from his father and furthered it throughout his life. He knew many herbs for numerous diseases. When he grew old he would take my oldest brother along and upon his death my brother inherited all his secrets. I left home when I was a young boy and was working on the

197

coast when my father died. Shortly afterwards I had my first epileptic attack. One night when I felt very lonely and upset, my father appeared to me in a dream. He took me by the hand and led me through a thick forest until we came to an open space. There he pointed to a tall tree and told me that its bark contained strong medicine against *kifafa*. He showed me how to prepare the remedy from the bark. "My son," he said before he disappeared, "I want you to help people who suffer from *kifafa*." When I woke up I could hardly wait for daylight before I started out to find the tree. I wandered around in the forest in a daze, until I came upon a clearing which resembled the place my father had shown me, and there was, indeed, the tall tree I had seen in my dream. I took some of its bark and hurried home to my village. When my brother saw that I had the bark and heard about my dream he realized that our father wanted me to be a medicine man. He taught me everything he knew about the treatment of *kifafa* and sent me to other medicine men to learn more. When I returned home after a year, people began to come to me for treatment of *kifafa*. Some I have been able to cure—others not, and among the latter, myself."

The medicine man stopped as if listening. But as it was still very early in the morning and everything remained quiet, he picked up a piece of bark and continued. "This is the bark of the tree my father showed me in the dream. I always use this medicine first. When boiled in water it produces a foam like the froth of saliva on the mouth of a convulsing person. The patient must drink large amounts of this brew. If he gets diarrhea and vomits, he will be cured. He has to vomit until he expels a lump of slime and blood. That is the toad of *kifafa*. We think there is a supernatural toad in the stomach of the patient. It has to come out or the patient will not be cured. The treatment, which lasts a few days, has to be repeated after a month, and again after six months. But several conditions must be met if the treatment is to be effective. The patient must start the treatment as soon as he contracts *kifafa*. If he waits until he has burns from falling into the fire the prospect of a cure is very poor. Then a bunch of roots, bulbs and leaves are cooked together with a chicken, and the whole family must eat of the stew. During the year of treatment, the patient must refrain from hard physical work. Drinking home brewed beer and other alcoholic beverages is forbidden and the patient should stay quietly at home avoiding anything that might be upsetting."

"It is very important to prevent *kifafa* and so many of my medicines are for the patient's relatives, to strengthen them against the *kifafa* spirit," the medicine man continued. "Certain dreams, especially those of being chased by wild animals, are forebodings that somebody in the family might come down with *kifafa*. A medicine man must be consulted and the right kind of medicine taken by the whole family. There is one dream in particular which is called 'the dream of *kifafa*' and if you ask the *kifafa* patients you will find that most of them have had this dream. The dreamer is about to wash himself. He pours water from a vessel over his shoulders with a feeling of pleasure. Suddenly he sees that the water turns red, like blood. He wakes up in a panic and might fall into convulsions right then. In any case he should hurry to get medicine against the dream." The medicine man picked up a root, the one with the repulsive smell. "This root is called *nefuzi*. It is hung by the bedside. Its bad smell will chase away the evil spirit of *kifafa* and prevent bad dreams from harming the sleeper."

The sun was now high in the sky and life began to awaken at the mission. The medicine man stood up and said he would have to leave. Before he bundled up his remedies he gave me the piece of bark from the tree his father had shown him in the dream and said it was his wish that I should take it with me to Europe when returning home. Maybe it could be made into tablets like the ones he got from me. Maybe his medicine could be of help to many patients suffering from epilepsy, even in Europe. He seemed satisfied when I put the piece in a box and promised that I would do what he asked. Then he slipped out and quickly went on his way before anybody had seen him. Later I had the bark analyzed in a pharmacological laboratory in Switzerland and it was indeed found to have anticonvulsive properties in animal tests.

The medicine man spent a few more early morning hours with me, each time taking care that nobody would see him coming or going. Of course I too did not mention his visits to anyone for fear that he would not return. What he told me helped me greatly in understanding the behavior of my *kifafa* patients and their families. Once he mentioned that his medicines are most effective at the time of the new moon. When I looked surprised he explained that *kifafa* was in some ways connected with the phases of the moon. This statement impressed me since I knew that the ancient Greek physician Hippocrates had taught that the frequency of seizures varied with the moon phase. Throughout the Middle Ages and until quite recently it was generally believed in Europe that epilepsy and mental disease were aggravated during the time of full moon ("lunatic"). However, the medicine man in Africa claimed that it was during the new moon that *kifafa* got worse. Nobody would consider treatment to be successful before at least three full phases of the moon had elapsed without attacks during new moon, he said. I had always been puzzled when patients pointed to the sky and spoke about the moon when explaining about their epileptic seizures. Phrases such as "Let us wait until the moon is starting to grow" or "I am all right because the moon is full" now became meaningful to me. Soon I caught myself watching the moon and was satisfied that the patient had the right dosage of anticonvulsant medication only if he came through the moonless nights without epileptic seizures. I gained the impression that the *kifafa* sufferers had indeed more attacks during the phase of the new moon. Maybe anxiety and fear can precipitate attacks. One thing is certain, that people without electricity are much more aware of the moonlight than we are. They fear the moonless nights when wild animals and all kinds of evil spirits lurk in the dark.

As time passed and people saw the effectiveness of my treatment and I learned to understand their reactions to

200

kifafa, tension eased. I noticed with amusement that the questions I used to ask the new *kifafa* patient and his family had been circulated among the people and the family would come well prepared for their first interview. As a matter of fact, our first meeting became a kind of ritual; I had to make sure I was asking the questions in the same order every time and that I did not forget any. By the satisfied or anxious expression on their faces I could tell whether I had followed the "rules" or not. The same thing happened with the medicine itself. I had collected a certain type of small medicine bottle and each patient was warned never to use the bottle for anything else but his pills and never to give of the medicine to anybody. The little bottle with its contents also became part of the ritual. The *kifafa* patients would carry it wrapped in their clothes like others did with their tobacco purse. At a certain hour the patient would unwrap the bottle and take his medicine. It became an important moment for everybody around. People began to fear that little bottle with its potent content. A great power must dwell in there, they inferred, since it could subdue the mighty *kifafa* spirit. I had asked the patients to place the bottle high up under the roof at night so that it would be out of the reach of children. From its niche above the bed the bottle with the medicine was believed to protect the sleeper from evil spirits and bad dreams. Like the bad smelling root of the medicine man it became a symbol of healing not only for the patient, but for the whole family as well.

As the number of patients seeking treatment for *kifafa* grew steadily, we could no longer find the time to handle them as well as the other patients every day. So we decided to set aside every Friday for *kifafa* patients and to close the dispensary for others on that day. The mission nurse and her helpers were then free to work with me, keeping record of the epileptic patients, their medicine and progress. Each patient was handed one week's supply of medication. Some who were seizure-free were given supplies for a whole month or more. At first we were quite nervous every Friday and expected some bad news. Would they all remember to come? Had some of them forgotten to take their medicine? Were they too ill to walk to the dispensary? To our great relief, however, most *kifafa* sufferers turned out to be remarkably reliable. Their fear of the *kifafa* spirit made them carefully follow my advice and the rules we had worked out and in case they themselves sometimes forgot to take the medicine their family was sure to remind them. Their cheerfulness and happy smiles, their never ending thankfulness and warm attachment to us made these Fridays unforgettable. We were never able to finish work until late at night, but nobody seemed to mind. People used to bring us small gifts such as eggs and chickens, fruit and rice. After they had checked in at the dispensary they would stay around on the lawn in front of the church exchanging news with jokes and laughter. The unique experience of being in the company of so many other recovering epileptics gave them a tremendous upsurge of self-confidence, and with a frankness they had never dared to display before, they would cheer at anybody who happened to pass by. Sometimes one or two of them would bring their drums and they would all join in singing and dancing. What a marvel to see these once so shy, sick and miserable people now sparkling with joy as they danced to the fast beats of their drums, perspiration glistening on their bodies. Bystanders and latecomers would join in; it was a feast for us all.

But the day had to come, the day I began to dread when I realized that I could not accept any more new *kifafa* patients. I spent long sleepless nights trying to figure out what to do and made up ambitious dreams of how I would help the people to build a village for the epileptics somewhere close to the dispensary. There would be receiving homes for newcomers where they and their families could stay until the epileptic was stabilized on medication. There would be land for gardens and many opportunities to learn handicraft skills so that they could become self-sustaining. Beautiful dreams I had! But the reality was that I had used up all my money and that the mission which had been so helpful was threatened to be inundated by *kifafa* patients. I could calculate that since each epileptic needed on the average two tablets a day and there were two hundred of them, the mission would have to come up with more than a hundred thousand tablets a year. That in itself was a formidable task for a mission in a remote mountain area, far away from the coast. I had hesitated for a long time to take a hard look at the reality of my undertaking because it meant that I would have to go back to Europe and raise funds and supplies for the continuing treatment of all these patients. I asked the medicine man whether there were still many *kifafa* sufferers in the tribe who had not yet contacted me and his answer frightened me. He claimed that the disease was on the increase and that numerous untreated cases were still tucked away in remote mountain villages. I knew I would have to leave, because as long as I was there, new patients would continue to arrive and ask for treatment. I hoped no additional pressure would be put on the mission once I was gone. With a heavy heart I assembled my helpers and together with the nurse explained to them why I would have to leave. They would have to keep the treatment center going until I could return with more money and supplies of medicine. The nurse would keep me informed by writing reports and I would continue to advise her. My departure would have to be kept secret to avoid an avalanche of anxious *kifafa* sufferers who would try to be started on treatment before I left. They listened with tears in their eyes and accepted the inevitable whether they fully understood it or not. The week before I left became a trial, especially the Friday. When the patients flocked around me as usual greeting me and touching me fondly, I felt like a traitor. They did not know that this would be our last meeting for a long time to come. How well I knew them all and how I had grown fond of them through our common struggle against *kifafa*. My last night turned into a sleepless nightmare. I could see them all, the *kifafa* patients who had so completely confided in me. Would they feel betrayed? *Was* I betraying them?

It was hard to carry the burden of my doubts alone, everything looked so dubious on that last night. Over-tired and sick at heart, I packed my things and sat down waiting for the landrover to pick me up in the early morning. When I heard it coming I rose from my heavy thoughts with a sigh and opened the door. And there, as if materialized out of the cold mist of dawn was a huge grey toad, sitting motionless where so often *kifafa* patients had waited for me in the morning. It looked at me with big black eyes, the spirit-toad of *kifafa*! For a moment I was frightened. We stared at each other. Who would be the winner—the spirit of *kifafa* which seemed bent on destroying a whole tribe, or I, who for the moment was compelled to retreat because of the sheer number of *kifafa* sufferers? The toad did not move. It looked ugly and to my weary eyes it seemed to grow until finally I pulled myself together. I would not succumb to superstitions. With determination I stepped over the slimy creature on my way to the waiting car. It marked the beginning of my long journey back to Europe.

21
Back in Europe

Nearly a year had passed since that day when I stepped over the *kifafa*-toad at the mountain mission in East Africa. I had not yet found a way to vanquish the beast, but neither had I given up fighting it. After a short holiday with my family in Norway, I went to Switzerland where I thought I would have the best chance to find support for my African plans. Professor Manfred Bleuler, chief of the university psychiatric hospital in Zurich, had for years shown great interest in my work in Africa and had supported it financially. As soon as he knew I was back in Europe, he offered me a position at the *Burgholzli* hospital.

Once I was established in my new job, Professor Bleuler encouraged me to work on my doctoral thesis under his supervision. I was to write about the medical, psychological, and social aspects of *kifafa*. He also used his influence to give me the opportunity of presenting the case of the African epileptics at scientific congresses and at meetings of charitable organizations. My presentations met with much interest and the humanitarian aspect of my work was fully recognized, but nobody offered financial support for the clinic at Mahenge. To my dismay I discovered that epilepsy held low priority in the health care planning of governments and international agencies. Epilepsy falls between the specialties of neurology and psychiatry. It is a stepchild of medicine and therefore institutions for epileptics usually suffer from a lack of funds.

Through the endeavors of Professor Bleuler, however, I received an invitation to present my *kifafa* treatment project to the World Health Organization in Geneva. Full of excitement I sat in the train on the way to Geneva, planning what I would say in front of the international experts. When I ascended the broad steps of the Palais des Nations it felt like a dream come true. I soon found myself seated at a large green table in a dark conference room. A dim light shone from a desk lamp standing beside the only other person present in the room. This was an elderly gentleman who, at that time, was in charge of Mental Health at the W.H.O. He seemed to hide behind a pair of dark glasses as he faced me across the table, and when he asked in a cold dry voice what I had to tell him, my confidence failed. Intimidated beyond recovery, I tried desperately to gather my thoughts. I had the feeling that I was addressing the green table, the empty chairs, the little lamp and the pair of dark glasses. While I was describing the plight of the *kifafa* sufferers and how a relatively small amount of money and outside help could create a self-sufficient center for epileptics with workshops, housing units and rehabilitation facilities both for the patients and for their families, the old man in the obscurity of the lampshade listened without moving or asking any questions. When I had finished, there was a long silence while I anxiously awaited his reply.

"Are you a specialist in neurology or psychiatry?" he asked. "No, but I..." "Well then, young lady," he interrupted me, and his voice sounded annoyed, "neither Professor Bleuler's recommendations nor your beautiful eyes will help you in this matter. Since there appears to be some virtue in your proposals, I suggest you come back to us when you are a specialist and have made a name for yourself. We may then consider lending you the umbrella of W.H.O." He called his secretary, dictated a few sentences to that effect and filed the note away in a thin folder upon which my name was written. "We are not discussing *me*!" I wanted to say. "What about all the epileptics in the meantime?" The hard face with the dark eyeglasses made further discussion impossible. Frustrated and humiliated, I ran down the steps I had climbed with so much hope. On my return trip to Zurich the disappointment changed to anger. I was going to show him. Even if it was to take many years, I would come back; and I would never let anybody put me down like that again.

When I told Professor Bleuler about my ill-fated expedition to W.H.O. he tried to cheer me up, discussing what else could be done. He suggested that I take part of my training at the Swiss Institute for Epileptics in Zurich, headed by his friend Dr. Landolt, an international authority on epilepsy. He said he would contact pharmaceutical companies to have them donate medication and funds for the epileptics in Mahenge. He spoke with such warmth and enthusiasm that I regained my self-confidence and exclaimed, "I am going to build the Treatment Center for *kifafa* even if I do not get any help from W.H.O.!" "That would mean spending many years in Africa," Professor Bleuler said after a thoughtful silence. "I wonder whether you are fully aware of the consequences for your own life if you embark upon such a project? You might jeopardize your professional career here in Europe, and if you excuse me for becoming personal, you would probably risk your chance of ever getting married, if this is of any concern to you." He added gently, "Remember you are not getting any younger, and believe me, there are few men who would be prepared to follow you to Africa for such a task." I looked at him anxiously. Consequences I had not thought of before now appeared very threatening to me. "What shall I do then? Of course I would want to marry and have a family, but I cannot just forget the epileptics I pledged to help. Physicians in tropical Africa say it is not possible to treat epileptics in remote areas.I have shown that it can be done. If I give up now, many epileptics in the African bush who otherwise would have a chance to start a new life will have to go on untreated and miserable." "True", Professor Bleuler said with a smile, "no doubt this task is important, but you must understand that it is by no means a matter of course that one puts one's life last for the sake of others. That is a matter of personal principle. I only want you to think it over carefully and not drift into a situation which you have not really planned and which might have serious consequences for your whole life."

I had to think about these words for a long time. Had my life in Africa not been that way? Drifting from one situation to the next, I had seldom taken time to reflect on my actions. Even coming to Zurich and starting training in psychiatry had been more an outgrowth of my work in Africa than part of my original intention.

Life as a resident psychiatrist at the Zurich University Clinic was not an easy one at a time when most of the modern medications were not yet available and there were indeed moments when I had doubts about continuing in this branch of medicine. At the *Burghölzli* the staff physicians still lived in the hospital just as Professor Bleuler and his father before him had done. Professor Bleuler's home was right there in the main building, and most of the residents in psychiatry had their rooms next to his suite. We were expected to make ward-rounds before and after the regular work hours, and the physician on call had to go through the whole hospital in the late evening before retiring for the night. Being used to the open spaces and the bright sunshine of Africa, the old hospital with its long corridors, dark rooms and locked doors appeared very oppressive to me. Here too the drama of life and death was acted out, but with a difference. When I wandered through the dark corridors at night, hearing shrieks and moans, as the orderly with the bundle of heavy keys unlocked one door after the other, I tried to ease the tension I felt by thinking of my friends in Africa. How this place would have frightened them! They would have thought that the whole hospital was full of menacing spirits and that many of the agitated patients would turn into wild animals at any moment.

208

The psychiatric orderlies accompanying me on the rounds reminded me of the faithful "dressers"I had worked with in Africa. Having worked in the jungle of mental suffering for years, these orderlies knew how to handle the patients entrusted to them. Friendly and calm, they stayed at my side, protecting me from agitated patients and tactfully suggesting to me, the beginner, how best to manage each individual case. Thanks to them I soon felt more comfortable. But among my colleagues I remained an outsider. I was not able to find my way back into the life of a modern European city. Even at social events I felt out of place.

Thinking of Professor Bleuler's words, I began to look closer at the men I met. I seemed to bore them with my never-ending preoccupation with Africa. Africa was like an obsession, like a fever in my blood. How could these European city dwellers understand the magic spell Africa casts upon those who have lived there? We obviously did not speak the same language, and I felt exceedingly lonely. Had it not been for Professor Bleuler, my fatherly friend, and the many letters I received from Africa, I might have lost myself in depressive brooding. Every Friday I saw before my inner eye the patients gather at the Mahenge Clinic to receive their medicine. Whenever the Clinic ran out of funds I sent part of my salary to the nurse. Her letters told me how well patients were doing and contained thankful notes from them which made up for any hardship I felt. One of the patients wrote:

Dear Doctor, I am very pleased to write you in order to inform you that my health and condition as regard to my ailments you know are very well progressing. I must try to identify to you my movements because of these tablets with the very precious treatments which must make me remain always thankful to you for carefully managing to care for my disease. I have disposed of this not very bright invention of a letter hereby presented obediently to you thus God may heed to what remains best for thanking you doctor. You being away from

Tanganyika is a straight sorrow especially to those depending thoroughly on you, like the poor lad as I am. Kindly present my best wishes to your parents, sisters and brothers and all your countrymen and women. Yours cordially. Amani.

Those charming letters from African schoolboys I used to get, reached me now even in Europe.

Dear doctor of mine, I am sure you won't remember me, if you only read this letter, but I will remind you that on the day before you left Mahenge for Europe, there were two young men who came to your office for a farewell. The young men asked for your address which you kindly handed to them. They also asked you to find girl friends for them in your country, whose request you kindly accepted. I'm one of those young men.

Well charming lady, it's now about a year since you left us. In due time I had a strong desire to write to you but I could unfortunately not find your address. Even though I did not lose your imaginary photograph which is still existing in my mind. I don't think that I'll have a minute of forgetting you one day till the end of my life. This afternoon I found your address in one of my books. Now imagine how lucky I have been. Unexpressable!

To state the fact, the friendship I introduced on that day wasn't for anybody in your country as I mentioned, but for yourself. I like you to be a pen pal of mine. I am a school boy who loves you. It's true that I've never come across a generous lady like you. You talk freely, you smile freely, you have initiative in your work. When you smile you look very pretty and I like you remaining that way all the time, and when you don't it makes no difference. I also like seeing you that way. Hullow, I appreciate that you are different from the other ladies, really exceptional. Should you prefer me remaining with only the imaginary photograph of yours I love you anyhow remembering how you look at me, sit, stand and walk.

210

My present address is as at the top of page one with the same name as at the bottom of page two.

When are you coming back again to Africa please? Yours in love, Francis.

Another schoolboy asked for my picture in a more sophisticated way. He wrote:

> Nowadays we are learning about culture, and we are trying to analyse Bantu culture. It is suggested as an hypothesis that the Bantu is not satisfied with abstract information or communication.
>
> He is more interested in concrete information given by a human being physically present than otherwise. Whether this hypothesis is in accordance with reality or not you might discover it when you come to Africa. But in fact this is the case with me. I would rather meet and talk with a person than write a letter to that person if meeting is possible and cheap. If meeting is not possible I cherish to read a letter from a person while being in possession of that person's picture. In short I am asking for one of your photos.
>
> At Mahenge last year we met for a very short time to *leave* each other. I hope one day we will meet for a long time to *live* and work together, where and when I hope, I shall give you many thanks for what you have done for me. Please, Yours Mawanja.

In the meantime the work on my thesis was progressing with difficulty. I often wondered how the people of Mahenge would react to my discussion of their *kifafa*-sufferers, and this doubt slowed down my writing until, one day, I hit upon the idea of writing to the Catholic bishop of Mahenge, himself a member of the Wapogoro tribe, asking for his advice. He sent me the following answer:

> Dear Doctor Louise, Thank you very much for your letter. Owing to lack of time I have been very late in an-

swering you. Today I am going to answer with this letter.

I am very impressed by your eagerness to help our poor epileptics. It is a pity that so far you have not found any encouraging responses to your appeal for financial help.

After getting your first letter I went to the different chiefs to get a clearer picture about how many epileptics there are in my diocese. One chief reported that there are about 150 more untreated epileptics in the Mahenge area. The other chiefs have not given their report as yet. It is very difficult to get exact numbers, because since the epileptics are shunned by other people, nobody likes to say that he or she is one. Even their near relatives help them to hide it until they can no more do so. Therefore only those who have epilepsy in a very advanced stage, and have repeated fits, are known by many people. It is my desire to help you as much as I can do. But it is a pity that my time is so much limited.

I am glad to hear that you are going to write a book about the Wapogoro and their *kifafa's*. I think you can write about the poverty of Wapogoro, their beliefs about *kifafa*, and their attitude towards those who have *kifafa*. Nobody will be offended if it is done in a manner which does not show that you intend to despise them for these weaknesses. Therefore you must be very careful in your description to avoid anything which may make Wapogoro think that you want to despise them. You may state the fact about their poverty, their beliefs about *kifafa*, and their attitude towards those who have *kifafa*. But then it would be good to point out that the cause of all these lies in the lack of facilities of improving their standard of living, and in lack of education about the causes of illness. Such a book will be all right, and every reasonable Mpogoro will be delighted to read it.

I think you must not hide the name of the place and of the tribe about which you are going to write, as there is no need to do so. Moreover, by hiding the name of the place and of the tribe about which you are going to write, you will, I think, sacrifice a very important element of the book, and needlessly. Therefore, I would advise you to describe everything clearly, courageously, but tactfully.

Wishing you good success, I pray God to bless your endeavour. Yours sincerely, Elias Mchonde, Bishop of Mahenge.

This answer encouraged me so much that I was able to complete the thesis in the next few weeks and then I left the *Burghölzli* hospital to start working at the Swiss Institute for Epileptics. On the first day, when Dr. Landolt took me around to show me the Institute and to introduce me to the epileptic patients, I felt deeply moved. Here was the model of what I had been hoping to create for my African patients. The epileptics lived in houses surrounded by fields and gardens. They worked together in workshops and on the farm and took care of the animals. They shared happiness and sorrow and assisted each other when one of them took a seizure. The Institute had a modern EEG laboratory where the patient's progress could be monitored closely and where Dr. Landolt and his co-workers conducted research into new treatment methods. Dr. Landolt was a shy and friendly man, loved by staff and patients alike. He became greatly interested in what I told him about *kifafa*.

There is no spirit-toad of epilepsy in modern Western society, he told me, but there is prejudice against the epileptics, reaching far back in time. The ancient Latin term for epilepsy, *morbus sacer*, a disease sacred as well as demoniac, reveals a deeply engrained ambivalent attitude toward those afflicted. In discussion with Dr. Landolt I found, to my surprise, that much of the magic belief surrounding epilepsy in Africa had also been part of European tradition until modern times. During the Middle Ages epilepsy had counted as one of the eight contagious diseases. Saliva of the convulsing epileptic had been thought of as especially dangerous. That epileptic attacks were influenced by the phases of the moon was firmly believed, just as it still is among the Wapogoro today; nor has

213

the suspicion that epilepsy might be sent by God as a punishment for sins quite disappeared among European peoples.

A few months after I had begun to work with the epileptics I was called to see the professor of pharmacology at the University of Zurich for whom I had brought medicinal herbs from Africa. With him was a representative of the pharmaceutical laboratories where the herbs had been analyzed. My heart began to béat faster when he broke the news that the bark I had received from the medicine man in Mahenge indeed possessed anti-epileptic properties. A decoction of the bark had been administered to test rats and had diminished the induced convulsions. Unfortunately the amount of material had been too small for further experiments. The researcher was now interested in obtaining a larger quantity. As much as a thousand pounds would be needed for conclusive analysis, he said. The question now was, would I be willing to undertake an expedition to gather the material if all expenses were paid by a pharmaceutical company?

For a while I was speechless. It was as if suddenly all the patients in Africa came alive inside my head, rushing forward, laughing, crying, calling and demanding. To my own surprise, my first feeling was apprehension rather than joy. Going to Africa right now? It would not be adventure any more — I knew that life too well. It was easy to dream about Africa in my comfortable apartment in Zurich — but to face all those problems again? What about my training which would have to be interrupted, and my well-paying job? I dropped my head in shame. Alas, there was the truth, the personal principle Professor Bleuler had talked about. I seemed to care more for myself than for the patients in Mahenge. Was it not the *kifafa*-toad I heard laughing in the distance? Finally I asked for time to think it over.

The following days I went around in a daze. Sometimes I felt happy and confident. What a triumph for my friend, the medicine man! He had told me that *kifafa* sufferers only needed to drink his decoction regularly for about a month to achieve relief from attacks for years. No modern medicine could match that. At other times I felt anxious and full of doubts. How could I get hold of a thousand pounds of the bark? Would the medicine man be willing to collect such an amount for me? What would the other tribesmen say? Would they not take offence at such a commercial undertaking? After all, the knowledge of medicinal herbs belonged to the sacred lore of the whole tribe. In any case it would take a long time to collect the material and while I was there in Mahenge many new epileptics would come for treatment and swell the number of patients attending the clinic. What should I do with them? How would I support them all? I recoiled from the many problems I knew I would have to face anew. And what about the loneliness? Had I not wept bitter tears in my bed there in Mahenge? Had I not stayed in my room at night so that the moon would not shine upon a lonely person?

One summer evening at the end of a workday I sat at my desk gazing forlorn out the window over the sunlit Lake of Zurich. "It is such a beautiful evening. I am driving out of town to the old castle of Rapperswil to take some pictures. Would you care to come along?" The friendly voice pulled me out of my painful loneliness. I turned around. An Austrian colleague who also worked at the Institute had come back to the office to pick up some books. We had never met outside the hospital, but I loathed the awful struggle that was going on in my mind and I accepted his invitation. We drove alongside the lake, but I was absentminded and could not catch on to the conversation. We stopped in Rapperswil at the bridge which traverses the lake at a narrow point. From here one has a marvelous view of the old castle. People were taking their evening stroll on the bridge. My colleague brought out his tripod and camera and we too set out across the bridge. In the middle of the bridge there was a space with flowers and benches. An amorous young couple was sitting on one, and my new friend, deciding that here was the best view of the castle, without the slightest embarrassment placed his tripod right in front of them. The young man looked up with a frown and said something in Italian. My colleague responded with a joke also in

215

Italian. They all had to laugh and the couple did not mind being photographed with the castle in the background. Watching from a distance I enjoyed the scene. The picturesque castle glowing in the setting sun was mirrored in the calm waters. And as I stood at the railing, smiling to myself, a new awareness came over me. Never had the colors of the sky appeared so warm, the songs of the birds sounded so gay and the sight of gold-rimmed clouds filled me with such content. In my heart I recognized that it all happened because I was not alone.

On the way back there was a good feeling between us and little by little I began to talk about what burdened me. I spoke of Africa and the difficult decision I would have to make. My colleague listened with interest and sympathy as he drove me back to Zurich. But when he had dropped me off and I was again alone in my apartment, I felt less inclined than ever to leave for Africa.

My indecision exhausted me and threw me into a depressed mood. When the day came for my answer, I knew I had to accept the proposal, but I did not feel happy about it. Just as I was leaving the Institute for the meeting with the pharmaceutical representative, my photographer-colleague caught up with me and quite simply asked whether it would be of any help if he came along to Africa? "I have some years of experience in neurology and psychiatry," he said "and since I have worked at the Institute here for over a year now I could easily arrange to be away for a few months." I looked at him in blank astonishment for I had never thought of such a possibility. It took me a long time to rearrange my thoughts. Slowly a feeling of great relief spread through me. I would not have to go back to Africa alone. Here was somebody willing to share responsibility with me, an experienced colleague whom I would be able to consult when facing difficult patients, someone to turn to when I was in trouble. I felt I could trust his judgement and count upon his friendship. "You really want to come with me to Africa?" — my voice was trembling with disbelief. "And I don't even know your first name!"

Epilogue

We did go to Africa together, my Austrian friend and I. Together we traveled through the worst rainy season I had seen and reached Mahenge after many adventures. The welcome we received in Kwiro was overwhelming. The *kifafa* patients gave us a big feast with dancing and singing. The photographic talent of my friend came to good use; I loved to show him the beauty of this African land and felt proud, as if I owned it all. The medicine man took us on safaris into the mountains to gather the barks and roots he used in the treatment of *kifafa*. He explained the names and properties of trees and herbs so well that we were able to identify the collected specimens botanically. The mission allowed us to dry the plants on the attic above the schoolgirls' dormitory, which, however, led to unexpected complications. The girls reacted with apprehension as the medicine man spread out his powerful remedies, and one night when the pungent smell of the *nefuzi* roots sifted down into their dormitory, they fled in panic. We had to send for the medicine man, and not before he had reassured the frightened girls would they go to bed again.

As I had predicted, new *kifafa* patients arrived daily. We had to examine all and screen them for admission. Together we re-organized the *kifafa* clinic and trained three Wapogoro girls to help the mission nurse care for the *kifafa* patients and their families. By the time we had to leave, the number of patients receiving regular treatment at our Center had swelled to over two hundred.

Our workday started at dawn and lasted until sunset, leaving us hardly any time for ourselves. Staying at a mission, we had to part at suppertime as my friend enjoyed the privilege of dining with the Fathers in the refectory. I envied him this opportunity of discussing African experiences with the missionaries while I had to eat alone in my little chamber. I used to watch for the lights to go out in the refectory; then I knew he would come back to be with me for a while before returning to his room at the Fathers' house. Now the mission was quiet and nobody disturbed us as we enjoyed the splendor of the tropical night.

It was a struggle to transport the dried plants the long way to the coast. The sacks had to be carried over flooded fields, canoed across swift rivers and driven on devastated roads, tightly packed in the back of our landrover. Most of the material had to be dried again in Dar-es-Salaam, where we spread it out on the sunbaked roof of the Archbishop's House. We felt great relief the day we finally managed to get the medicine man's cargo through the customs and shipped off to Europe. Unfortunately, our efforts to contribute to the development of a new antiepileptic agent out of the traditional African pharmacopeia were in vain. Chemical isolation of the effective principles turned out to be uneconomical for manufacturing and the pharmaceutical company finally lost interest.

We had a few relaxing days before we left East Africa. I thoroughly enjoyed them and had no objections when my friend took me to an Indian jeweller to choose our engagement rings. We married the same year and shortly afterwards emigrated to Canada where we made our home.

218

Throughout the years we kept alive the *kifafa* clinic in Mahenge, supporting it financially and consulting with the nurse on each case. We succeeded in supplying the patients with medication through the help of our friend Al Elliott of the pharmaceutical company Elliott-Marion of Canada. Encouraged by our Canadian friends, we have continued to attract the attention of humanitarians to the plight of the African epileptics and to create international awareness of the possibilities of treating and rehabilitating those afflicted with an otherwise disabling condition. At the Epilepsy International Symposium held in Vancouver in 1978 our presentation on *kifafa* and the factors accounting for its relatively high prevalence met with renewed interest and rekindled our hope for the eventual realization of a comprehensive treatment program for all sufferers from epilepsy in Africa.

PRINTED IN USA

Africa
250 miles

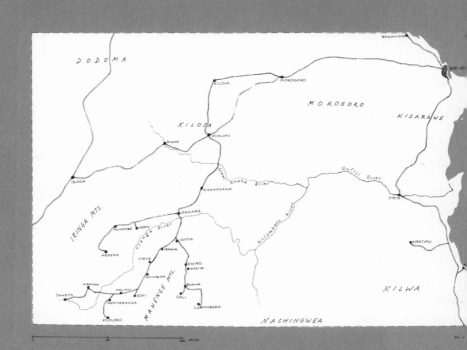